RESISTANCE
(AT ALL COSTS)

ALSO BY KIMBERLEY STRASSEL

The Intimidation Game: How the Left Is Silencing Free Speech

RESISTANCE (AT ALL COSTS)

HOW TRUMP HATERS ARE BREAKING AMERICA

KIMBERLEY STRASSEL

TWELVE

New York   Boston

Twelve
Hachette Book Group
1290 Avenue of the Americas, New York, NY 10104
twelvebooks.com
twitter.com/twelvebooks

First published in hardcover and ebook by Twelve in October 2019

First Trade Paperback Edition: October 2020

Twelve is an imprint of Grand Central Publishing. The Twelve name and logo are trademarks of Hachette Book Group, Inc.

The publisher is not responsible for websites (or their content) that are not owned by the publisher.

The Hachette Speakers Bureau provides a wide range of authors for speaking events. To find out more, go to www.hachettespeakersbureau.com or call (866) 376-6591.

Library of Congress Cataloging-in-Publication Data has been applied for.

ISBNs: 978-1-5387-0179-9 (trade paperback), 978-1-5387-0178-2 (ebook)

Printed in the United States of America

LSC-C

10 9 8 7 6 5 4 3 2 1

To the memory of my father, Mike Strassel

CONTENTS

INTRODUCTION

Political pundits learn early the risk of making predictions, but I will make one here: The reaction to this book—at least among some quarters—will prove its point.

The election on November 8, 2016, of Donald J. Trump to the presidency of United States unleashed many changes, though among the most enduring will be the rise of "the Resistance." Loosely defined, these are the legions of Americans who were resolutely opposed to the election of Trump, and who remain angrily determined to remove him from office. They come in every shape and size—Democrats, Republicans, ardent leftists, moderate suburbanites, brainwashed millennials—but they share one thing in common. They view everything to do with Trump in black-and-white morality. You either hate the man, or you are as bad as the man.

There is, in fact, a reason the subtitle of this book refers to "Trump haters" rather than "Trump critics." Many thoughtful Americans, and many thoughtful political writers, have issues with our 45th president—myself included. But the critics have also worked to do that very hard thing of judging Trump via the same lens they have judged past presidents. They praise him when he gets things right. They criticize him when he gets things wrong. This is the usual and long-held method of political accountability.

But the "haters" can't abide nuance. To the Resistance, any praise—no matter how qualified—of Trump is tantamount to American betrayal. And by extension, any criticism of the Resistance is equally heretical. If you are a Trump hater, this is an excellent way of shutting down challenges to your tactics or arguments. But it's a rotten way of furthering public debate, and the ensuing vacuum of meaningful discussion has already led the Resistance to overindulge. It is now engaging in behavior that is proving far more corrosive to our institutions and rule of law than anything of which it has accused the president.

Indeed, the claim that Trump marks some new or existential threat to the United States is hard to make in light of history. America has had many presidents who attracted deep loathing while in office, even from members of their own party. Not a few historians have made the comparison between Trump and Andrew Jackson, the nation's seventh chief executive. Jackson was combative and passionate, prone to fits of rage. He believed himself "the people's president," and that he was therefore justified in aggressive use of his powers. His critics—which included a lot of polite society and the press—decried him as a racist, of lacking the intelligence and temperament for office, and of engaging in patronage and personal enrichment. Opponents warned of the imminent demise of a young nation under a "dictator" and "tyrant"—a man they derided as "King Andrew." Yet Jackson also remains one of the more influential presidents. And obviously, the nation endured. While Trump has certainly brought a new and impolitic feel to the office of the presidency, the claims that he is a despot are simply false.

Notwithstanding some of his more flippant proposals, his presidency has, in fact, been remarkably rule bound. Unlike his predecessor, he has not governed by executive orders. He has dramatically *reduced* the size of federal government—not *expanded* it. He has appointed judges on the basis of their fidelity to the clear language of the Constitution and law. Despite shrieks of a budding autocracy, the 2018 midterms resulted in a normal, peaceful Democratic takeover of the House—nary a tank to be seen in the streets.

It is instead the reaction to Trump that is new and alarming, and that threatens to leave enduring marks. The term the haters have chosen for themselves—the Resistance—says it all. Throughout history, political resistance movements have existed to undermine occupying powers, as the French Resistance did in response to Nazi Germany. The very word suggests illegitimacy—a movement organized against an authority that has no right to rule. Yet whatever your views of Donald Trump, he won his election fair and square, under an Electoral College that has governed our system from the start.

The mind-set nonetheless explains how the Resistance has gone so far off the rails. Those who view their targets or their actions as illegitimate view themselves as justified in taking any action necessary to get rid of the occupier. Whether that be turning the awesome powers of the Department of Justice and the FBI against an unconventional presidential campaign, or ambushing a Supreme Court nominee with uncorroborated sexual-assault allegations, or using the impeachment process for political retribution, the Resistance views itself in the right.

But these actions aren't right. In a poker match, one player might not like the look of the other, or his taunts, or his aggressive play. But that doesn't give him the right to cheat—to slip an extra ace up his sleeve or mark cards. This has been the behavior of the Resistance leaders, and it has already caused harm to vital institutions. It is nothing short of alarming that huge swathes of the country no longer trust the Justice Department or the FBI to administer equal justice. Or that, according to a 2018 *Axios* poll, 72% of Americans believe that "traditional, major news sources report news they know to be fake, false or purposely misleading"—including 92% of Republicans and 79% of independents. Or that the Ninth Circuit Court of Appeals has felt compelled to rebuke anti-Trump district court judges for exceeding their powers. Or that 2020 Democratic presidential candidates campaigned on proposals to destroy some of our most basic aspects of U.S. democracy—from the Electoral College to the Senate filibuster.

So back to that prediction. This is not a book about Donald Trump, per se. There are lots of books about the Donald—some fawning, some reasonable, tons critical. Entire vats of ink have gone into analyzing his every action or non-action and predicting what each means for this nation. That area is well covered. Nor is this a book about the many millions of Americans who passionately, even understandably, dislike Donald Trump—but who remain committed to rule of law, dignity in politics, and principled opposition.

This is instead a book about the more radical elements of the Resistance, and how their reaction to Trump is causing significant damage to our institutions and political norms. It will certainly note the role Trump has played, to the extent he often drives his rivals crazy and has at times helped provoke their overreaction. But the subject here is the behavior of other side—the fringe of his opposition.

And yet I predict that for the sin of writing a book that is not unrelentingly, remorselessly, and absolutely critical of Trump, the Trump haters will attempt to portray this as some sort of Trump apologia. In doing so, they prove yet again that the truest haters aren't interested in debate or ideas or in restoring "norms"—as they claim—but only in engulfing the Trump administration in flames, and tarring and feathering as many of their critics as possible.

This pigeonholing isn't new space for that class of writers that I consider thoughtful "critics." For years now, the *Wall Street Journal* editorial page, under the leadership of Paul Gigot, has worked to provide fair and insightful analysis of the Trump administration, measured against our long-standing belief in "free markets, free people." Plenty of other right-of-center (and even some left-of-center) publications seek to do the same. We are often critical of Trump's manner and policies. But none of this counts for much among the Resistance, who instead cast any praise of the Trump administration—or criticism of their own behavior—as evidence of toadyism and propaganda, and who thereby (and self-servingly) seek to delegitimize broader arguments.

But if there is no room for a book that seeks to look as critically at the overreaction to Trump as at Trump himself, we as a civil society are lost. Trump will be in office for at most eight years. We will be living with the wreckage of the Resistance for much longer.

RESISTANCE
(AT ALL COSTS)

CHAPTER 1

VIVE LA RÉSISTANCE

Some say there are five stages of grief; some seven. For the Resistance—those unhappy Americans so bitterly opposed to the election of Donald J. Trump—there were only ever two: denial and anger. It's been an epic psychological fail, one with grave consequences for the country.

The denial stage was at least short-lived. I witnessed its immediate form at the election party I hosted at my Virginia home that November 8, 2016. I love anyone who loves politics (and a good party), so we played host to guests of every political persuasion: Clinton supporters, Trump supporters, and even one poor soul still pining for Ron Paul. I was busy flitting inside for drinks, outside to where we'd erected a TV projection screen, and back to my computer to compare notes with *WSJ* colleagues about what had become a surprisingly tight race. On one such run I suddenly noticed small groups of Trump supporters staring avidly at the screen. I noticed an equal number of Clinton supporters drifting—dazedly, confusedly—toward cars. It was around midnight, and reality had hit: Hillary Clinton could not win. "President Trump," murmured one Clinton supporter as I wished her safe travels. "It's inconceivable. It can't happen."

It did happen, and for the most part, denial faded. The more radical anti-Trumpers would, of course, continue to deny

Trump's legitimacy. Some rolled out the left's favorite complaint: the Electoral College. Trump had lost the majority vote, they said, and therefore Hillary *should* be president. Tell that to the Founders. Days and weeks after the inauguration, anti-Trumpers would seize on a yet more explosive argument for why Trump was not lawful: He had colluded with Russians to "steal" the election. But that conspiracy came later.

At the time, most Americans just geared up for the Trump inauguration. On one side was the Trump base, wild with joy that their candidate had proven the media and elites decidedly wrong. In the middle, a crucial number of voters who had pulled the lever for Trump, albeit reluctantly, and only because they would not tolerate another President Clinton. Also in the middle, Clinton supporters who were disappointed—but not unhinged—by the result. And finally, on the other end, a solid mass of Trump haters who had already decreed the president-elect a racist and a dictator, and who in a few short days of Trump's election would become, officially, "the Resistance."

They were fueled by that second stage, anger, and it was something to behold. Within hours of Clinton's concession, anti-Trumpers had taken over the streets, engaged in candlelight vigils, marches, riots. Crowds seethed around the Trump Tower in downtown Chicago. Demonstrations broke out in every major U.S. city, from Los Angeles to Dallas to Minneapolis to New York. People wept. People wailed. Anti-Trump protestors in Oakland, California, threw Molotov cocktails and M-80 firecrackers at police. Angry individuals hoisted banners that read "Time to Revolt" or "Make America Smart Again." Portland, Oregon, protestors took over the city for most of a week, blocking highways, delaying buses, vandalizing businesses and cars. One anarchist justified the violence to *The Oregonian* by explaining that no one should expect "black youth" to be "peaceful" when "Nazis are going to kill them." Twitter was besieged with hashtags: #nevermypresident; #notmypresident; #StillWithHer.

Cornell students gathered for a "cry-in." The University of Kansas urged students to make use of therapy dogs. The University of Michigan comforted distraught students with coloring books and Play-Doh.

The nation's liberal punditocracy meanwhile took to their computers. A rare few approached the task with almost touching normality. Eric Frazier, a self-described progressive editor for the *Charlotte Observer*, described his disappointment with the results, but suggested folks "move on." "Congratulate a Trump supporter," he said, and "accept defeat." There were "rational reasons why Hillary Clinton lost," including that the "economic pain" of Trump's "rural, white blue-collar base is very real." "Remember," he wrote, "it wasn't going to be the end of the world no matter who won."

Few agreed. Timothy Egan of the *New York Times* explained in his post-election column that he hadn't "felt this way since the nuns told our second-grade class that John F. Kennedy had been assassinated." *The New Yorker*'s David Remnick penned a piece titled "Presidential Election 2016: An American Tragedy," in which he decried the triumph of "nativism, authoritarianism, misogyny and racism," and, of course, brought up George Orwell. "It is impossible to react to this moment with anything less than revulsion and profound anxiety," he lamented. Paul Krugman, the *NYT*'s reliably incorrect economist, offered his own apocalyptic prediction. "We are very probably looking at a global recession, with no end in sight."

Krugman's prediction turned out to be among the least hysterical. Trump critics declared an end to democracy as we knew it, under an administration primed to commit every manner of crime, abuse, and offense. No claim was too wild. Trump would strip women, the LGBT community, and voters in general of their rights. He'd deport the Dreamers and block liberal groups from providing any women's services. Progressives predicted Trump would encourage reprisals against Muslim citizens.

Rolling Stone quoted an anonymous "prominent rights leader" explaining that Trump would probably use "surveillance power to go after critics." The same piece quoted ACLU executive director Anthony Romero bracing for a "full-blown 'civil liberties crisis.'" Other outlets suggested Trump already had a "secret enemies list," à la Nixon, and that he'd turn the state on those targets. Not a day passed when Trump was not compared to Hitler, a fascist, a monster, or a bigot. Columnists further fanned fears by noting that there was no "check" on the budding autocrat. As Egan explained in his initial post-election column: "Those who think Trump can be contained, or trained by seasoned K street hacks to act reasonable, are deluding themselves. . . . The Republicans will control everything, including the Supreme Court. Washington is theirs, with minimal checks and balances."

These warnings didn't fade. As recently as June 2019, presidential candidate Joe Biden in Iowa explained that Trump "poses three fundamental threats to America" and that one of these was to our "democracy." "Everywhere you turn, Trump is tearing down the guardrails of democracy," said Uncle Joe. "We're at a moment when we need to reset constitutional norms in this country."

* * *

People didn't like Trump the man, true. It was outrageous to the left that the real estate baron they had written off as a joke and an imbecile had won, and had done so by appealing to the very fly-over America the elite holds in such contempt. Add to this Donald J. Trump's almost unparalleled ability to infuriate his opponents. It isn't just his blunt, impolitic style. Over the decades, the press and liberal elites had grown accustomed to setting the rules of the game, scolding Republicans who failed to play by them, and accepting the ensuing apologies. Trump, infuriatingly, refused to play.

But what few on the left or in the media would acknowledge is that this anger also came from something completely aside from Trump. It was a seething fury over *losing in general*—in particular over losing such a consequential election.

Every presidential election matters—but some matter more. The 2016 election mattered lots, coming as it did after eight years of Barack Obama's experiment with liberal government. The 44th president had proven one of the more radical in modern history, relentlessly pushing to expand the size of federal government, regulate or take over private industry, and stock the courts with activist judges. A Republican Congress had nonetheless forced him to do much of this via regulation and executive order—all of which could be undone.

Democrats had soaring ambitions for a Hillary Clinton presidency. She would cement Obama's gains and put the nation irrevocably on a path to progressive enlightenment. Obama had given the federal government sweeping new control over private health care; Clinton would use anger over the resulting soaring prices to pivot to true, government-run care. Obama erected a hulking new bureaucracy to micromanage the energy and finance sectors; Clinton would cement those regulations for eight more years, making it impossible for Republicans to dismantle them. Obama raised taxes on the wealthy; Clinton would make that the new norm and continue to grow the size of government. A Clinton administration would protect Obama's legally dubious moves: the Paris Climate Accord, his executive immigration orders, his crackdown on religious freedom. And the granddaddy of ambitions? The Supreme Court was finally, tantalizingly up for grabs. A Republican Senate had blocked Obama from putting his nominee, Merrick Garland, in the seat of the recently deceased Antonin Scalia. Clinton would see that nomination through. For the first time since Nixon, there would be five reliably liberal justices on the Court, potentially more if another conservative retired or died during a Clinton presidency.

Trump's victory demolished this dream. And the left's rage was against everyone and everything. It was furious at its own side—that the party had been so foolish as to settle for its heir apparent, Hillary Clinton, and close its eyes to her failures and baggage. A growing and ascendant progressive wing of the party was still angry that the Democratic National Committee had rigged the primary against its favorite, Bernie Sanders.

It was furious with Republicans overall—particularly that the GOP had blocked Obama from doing more in his time in office. "Dear people who spent eight years demonizing Obama at every turn and are now tweeting me to 'give Trump a chance' on day 1: Trust is earned," declared American actor Seth MacFarlane. Democrats raged over the Garland nomination, throwing it out as an immediate reason for why the party should deny Trump cooperation on anything.

The left was furious at any group or body that it felt might have played a role in allowing Trump to happen. That included pollsters, who had misgauged the depth of Trump support and led Clinton into false security; the FBI, which had briefly reopened the probe into Clinton's private server right before the election, potentially depressing her turnout; women, for the crime of supposedly voting against their own self-interest; and, of course, the media, for giving Trump so much air time. Anti-Trumpers poured particular venom on CBS executive chairman and CEO Les Moonves, who during the campaign bluntly celebrated Trump's effect on TV income and ratings: "It may not be good for America, but it's damn good for CBS," he told a conference in February 2016.

And the rage only increased as the election results sank in. It suddenly crystallized for Democrats not just that they'd lost, but just how true it was that Trump *wasn't* the typical Republican president. Republicans always run on lower taxes, fewer regulations, and smaller government. But the left and the media had become good over past decades at browbeating Republican candidates and presidents out of a truly conservative agenda. They'd barrage them with criticism in sensitive policy areas like the environment, or health care, or poverty programs, and the GOP would step back. Republican leaders changed things, but only slowly and around the edges.

Trump, Democrats realized in horror, really didn't give a toss what anyone thought of him. Moreover, he seemed to care deeply about fulfilling his campaign promises. The Paris Climate Accord? Gone. All those climate-change rules? Gone. Obamacare? Trump would repeal it, if at all possible. The judiciary? Candidate Trump's 2016 list of potential Supreme Court nominees included an all-star roster of textualist jurists and thinkers. And as the *NYT*'s Egan morosely pointed out, Trump had also carried to victory a Republican House and Senate. He had the allies to pass his agenda. Democrats hadn't just lost their fairy-tale castle in the sky; they'd landed a dragon.

The left's hatred of Trump the man combined with its fury over its loss to create an epic level of rage. We have no way of knowing whether this anger has any equal in history. What we do know is that history had never before provided the twenty-first-century tools that would allow this fury to explode and grow and endure. Social media gives Trump critics the ability to immediately organize and to perpetuate a state of permanent anti-Trump outrage. Twenty-four-hour cable stations, flanked by hundreds of Internet outlets, seize on every accusation—collusion, corruption, incompetence—and stoke and push the charges into every home, transforming "news" into a new form of political takedown.

And within days, the anger turned into a formal, committed movement. Indeed, the speed with which the idea of resisting Trump morphed into an official "Resistance" movement was remarkable. At first, it was just liberal polemicists decrying the election results. *New York Times* columnist Charles Blow, in a November 10 column titled "America Elects a Bigot," lamented that America had chosen a man who "appeared in pornos" and "boasted of assaulting women." He concluded: "I respect the presidency; I do not respect this president-elect. I cannot. Count me among the resistance."

Perhaps the first post-election formalization of the term came with a viral video from liberal personality Keith Olbermann, via *GQ*'s website. He predicted: "At some juncture soon there will be the resistance. Those of us who warned against and pleaded against and fought against this madness will find avenues for dissent, which will have enough support to at least impede this monster." He added his own twist on Churchill (with no apologies to the conservative hero): "We shall fight online. We shall fight in the press and on television. We shall fight on the street corners of public opinion. We shall never surrender." Within a week of the election, the *San Francisco Chronicle*'s political writer, Joe Garofoli, had given the word a capital "R." He called on Americans to "unfurl out of the fetal position, stop moaning to your Facebook friends, and do something positive if you're seething or freaked out or scared by the prospect of President-elect Donald Trump." What would that be? Garafoli explained: "Organizers are urging anti-Trumpers to join the Resistance."

Join they did. By Inauguration Day, that Resistance was fully organized. And it was on that day that it became clear that the Resistance was something all its own and particularly corrosive to democracy.

I'd agreed on Inauguration Day to provide commentary for CBS News, which involved getting across D.C. in a car. That meant picking our way through the inaugural crowds. I saw plenty of concerned citizens calmly walking with anti-Trump signs. They were engaging in the kind of peaceful political protest that is a hallmark of American society and of which we should generally be proud.

But I also saw people smashing car windows, racing in mobs after anyone in a MAGA hat, screaming taunts and insults at the media. They were the folks already holding the "Impeach" signs and promising they would not stop until Trump was forcibly re moved from office. The claims of illegitimacy, the scorched-earth tactics—that's the official Resistance.

* * *

And that is why it is so important to make distinctions. Here's an important one: Not everyone who passionately dislikes Trump is part of the radical Resistance. Plenty of average Americans don't want this president and are committed to seeing him leave office. But they want to see that happen via the ballot box in 2020; they are not willing to break all the rules to get an earlier result.

Contrast the tactics of the Resistance, for instance, to its putative forbearer—the Never Trump movement. Trump had faced down his own GOP mutiny in the months leading to and following his nomination. The Never Trumpers counted among their ranks every type of conservative: grassroots activists, pundits, faith leaders, politicians, former Republican officials. And Trump had given each of them an ostensible reason to oppose his nomination.

In the course of a year's campaign, the real estate mogul had deployed some shocking language and behavior. He'd mocked a disabled reporter. He'd taunted his primary rivals—making fun of Carly Fiorina's face, calling Jeb Bush "dumb as a rock," and ridiculing the size of Marco Rubio's ears. Some voters—many who'd watched Trump in his reality TV days—wrote it off as Trump-shtick. Others found it refreshing, an antidote to too-polished politicians. But for many Republicans, it was a mark on his character.

He'd rattled a number of Republicans with his policy proposals, particularly the biggies of trade and immigration. The GOP had long hailed itself the free-trade party. Trump, while claiming to be a free-trader, railed against pacts that he claimed were a continued "rape of our country." Republican leaders for years had pushed for a grand immigration bargain and a path to citizenship for millions of illegal immigrants. Trump came down on the side of local officials and base voters who instead wanted more border security, and he promised to build a "great wall."

Defense hawks worried he might completely withdraw troops from global hot spots. Law-and-order conservatives worried that Trump, like Obama, would rule via executive order or presidential decree. Whole crowds of Republicans noted that he'd only recently been a Democrat and worried he'd govern like one.

The point is: Whether you agreed with them or not, most Never Trumpers had principled reasons for their opposition, which stemmed from their own deeply held views of conservatism. All this meanwhile came at a time when Trump was still a relatively unknown quantity, and as Republican primary voters were bickering angrily over *all* their candidates.

Yet the problem for Never Trumpers was that other thing they all claimed to deeply believe in: democracy. In April 2016, Trump was close to locking up the 1,237 delegates needed to win the nomination. News broke that his two remaining rivals, Texas Senator Ted Cruz and Ohio Governor John Kasich, had teamed up with the sole goal of denying Trump the nomination and forcing a contested convention. Some Never Trumpers also started working to convince delegates in states Trump had won to break their pledges and vote against him at the convention. These headlines infuriated many Republican primary voters, who felt elites were rigging the game. And it backfired. On the eve of the crucial Indiana primary in May, a *Wall Street Journal*-NBC-Marist poll found that 58% of Indiana primary voters disapproved of the Cruz-Kasich effort. As CNN commentator Marc Lamont Hill observed: "Voters feel like Donald Trump is being now thwarted, he is being blocked, he is being obstructed." Prior to all this, Cruz had polled competitively in Indiana. By the end of voting, Trump had crushed him by 17 percentage points. The Texan dropped out of the race.

And that was pretty much the end of the Never Trump movement. A few holdouts made a last stab at thwarting Trump's bid
at the August convention, but the effort went nowhere. While
Democrats were more than willing to rig their own primary
to crown Hillary over Bernie, Republican leaders ultimately rejected such tactics—to their credit. To do otherwise was un-
democratic and would provoke a voter backlash. As we at the
WSJ editorial page wrote when Trump wrapped up the nomination: "GOP voters made the ultimate decision, and that deserves
some respect unless we're going to give up on democracy." The
ultimate list of Trump convention speakers ranged from House
Speaker Paul Ryan to faith leader Jerry Falwell Jr. to Silicon Valley
entrepreneur Peter Thiel to *Duck Dynasty* star Willie Robertson.
And in the months and years since the convention, the vast majority of original Never Trumpers have cautiously accepted the
president, whether out of admiration for (or relief over) his conservative agenda or (ironically) in response to what they now
view as unfair attacks from his opponents.

The Resistance, from the start, has been something very different. True, it still counts among its ranks some prominent
conservatives who continue to reject a Trump presidency. But
they are the misfits in this movement. Whereas the original Never
Trumpers were concerned Trump would *destroy* conservatism,
the vast majority of the new Resistance hate Donald Trump for
embracing conservative policies. And whereas the original Never
Trumpers agreed to let democracy take its course, the Resistance
continues to work to immediately destroy his presidency.

Which brings us to the second major distinction: Within the
Resistance, there are leaders, and there are followers. And they
are not necessarily in that movement for the same reason.

The vast majority of those Americans who blithely refer to
themselves on social media as part of the Resistance are the
followers. They are daily whipped into frenzies by the steady
stream of accusations against Trump—the claims of his racism,

misogyny, treason, authoritarianism, and more. Some are politically aware, though blinded by their hate. Some have no clue of the facts, but are willing to believe anything (think: most snowflake college students).

But it's the leaders of the Resistance who are doing the damage, and are the primary focus of this book. They are a loosely gathered collection of Democratic politicians, political operatives, big-name pundits, news organizations, and well-funded activists. For as much as these folks legitimately dislike Trump, they are also smart enough to know that the president is not a Russian spy, or a racist, or a tyrant. They nonetheless continue to every day decry him in the most over-the-top and relentless ways possible. They do this for a simple reason: It benefits them.

First and foremost, a politics of fear allows them to gin up the masses, to whip those Resistance followers into a hysteria that pays handsomely—literally. Within days of Trump's inauguration, liberal special interest groups were fund-raising like mad off their dire predictions of his presidency. "Join the Resistance: Stop Donald Trump's Attacks on the Environment. Donate Now!" read one e-mail from Friends of the Earth in November 2016. In February 2017, the *Washington Times* reported that the Sierra Club was bragging its donations had swelled by 700 percent since the November election, compared to the same period a year earlier. Every traditional organization got in on the act—civil rights groups, environmental organizations, labor unions, pro-choice outfits.

Bigger, umbrella fund-raising organizations also cashed in. The Sixteen Thirty Fund is a left-leaning group that collects money from donors, and then "sponsors" liberal projects. In 2016, when Obama was still president, it raised $21 million. Contributions in 2017, Trump's first year in office, nearly quadrupled to $79 million.

The fear-mongering opportunity was so huge that Resistance leaders rushed to start up new nonprofits. Democracy

Forward—whose board includes Clinton's 2016 campaign chair-man, John Podesta—was launched with a mission of fighting Trump administration "corruption" in court. A former Obama official started American Oversight, a "Freedom of Information Act litigator investigating the Trump administration." Groups like Demand Justice were set up to oppose Trump judicial nomina-tions. The money continues to pour in.

Resistance slogans have proven equally lucrative for Demo-cratic politicians running for election. Anti-Trump rhetoric has fueled massive donations to political campaigns, starting with special elections in 2017, up through this 2020 election cycle. Democratic candidates for Congress in 2018 raised more than $1 billion, breaking records and swamping Republicans. Beto O'Rourke alone raised an extraordinary $80 million in his (ul-timately doomed) quest to unseat Texas Republican Senator Ted Cruz.

Resistance leaders have also used their nonstop Trump hate to mobilize volunteers and voters for Democratic causes. In October 2018, *Time* ran a piece titled "How the Anti-Trump Resistance Is Organizing Its Outrage." The story laid out how Resistance types were enlisting average Americans, fueled by anti-Trump fervor, to do their bidding. "Hundreds of thousands of volunteers, allied with thousands of autonomous groups, are doing the grunt work of propelling their neighbors to the polls, using tactics tailored to their communities. Suburban moms are knocking on doors in North Carolina battlegrounds; racial-justice organizers in Georgia are mobilizing black voters in churches and restaurants; college students in Pennsylvania are using social me-dia to reach new voters. In Texas, immigrant-rights activists are helping Latino voters get their paperwork in order. Teenage gun-safety advocates from Florida are on bus tours to register other newly eligible voters." An NBC News piece by Republican strate-gist Evan Siegfried in October 2018 laid out how all this was helping Democrats rack up voter registrations in key areas. "In

Iowa, 2018 voter registrations so far are double what they were at the same point in 2014. Even more telling is the partisan break-down: Democrats added 23,064 new members so far this year and Republicans only 1,636."

More broadly, Resistance leaders discovered the benefits of conflating Trump with his policies, as a way of delegitimizing the entire conservative agenda. Here's one way it works: A Resistance leader will call Trump ignorant and evil, but in the same breath also note that Trump believes in so-and-so policy. Ergo, said policy is ignorant and evil. In a November 26, 2018, column, the same *NYT* economist, Paul Krugman, decried the Trump administration as "anti-objective-reality." Trump and Republicans suffered from "sheer depravity" and engaged in "tough guy posturing." Mr. Krugman also tossed in the terms "greed, opportunism, and ego." It turns out the actual subject of the column was GOP climate change "denial." Only in the age of Trump can liberals write off those who question man-made global warming as morally "depraved."

Trump gives Resistance leaders new ways to demean and un-dercut their entire opposition. A particularly nasty claim is that Trump and his election somehow prove that conservatives as a whole are vile. Amy Goodman, the host of the liberal *Democracy Now!* news program, wrote at the end of 2016 that "Trump's campaign was overtly racist, and this seems to have motivated a terrifying number of voters." Got that? People didn't come out to vote for Trump because he promised lower taxes or less regu-lation or better judges. They did it because they hate minorities, according to the Resistance.

Resistance politicians have made an art of the same sort of guilt-and-dismissal by association. This was California Senator Kamala Harris in the days following the Trump election victory: "One side believes it is okay to demagogue immigrants, has pro-posed unrealistic plans to build a wall, and is promising to break up families by deporting millions of people. The other side believes in respect, justice, dignity and equality as part of an approach to bring millions of people out of the shadows." Again, every Republican, by virtue of voting for Trump, is against respect, justice, dignity, and equality.

Trump has also provided Resistance leaders new avenues for going after long-hated targets. In March 2019, *The New Yorker*'s Jane Mayer, infamous among liberal attack journalists, penned an 11,000-word screed against Rupert Murdoch and Fox News. [Disclaimer: Murdoch owns the *WSJ*.] There is nothing new in the left bashing conservative media outlets or bashing their owners. But Mayer had a new hook for her hit piece: Her article claimed Fox News served as "Trump TV," and her piece sought to explain how Fox had devolved from simply being "partisan" to instead being a full-time "propaganda" outlet for the Trump autocracy.

Finally, casting Trump as a dictator or racist or homophobe gives Resistance leaders cover to engage in behavior that would never have been tolerated in political times past. They accuse Supreme Court nominees of rape. They break Senate committee rules. They breach government regulations and even statutes (see all those leaks of classified information). They spend two years telling us to wait for the results of special counsel Bob Mueller's report, then ignore the results of Bob Mueller's report. They cheapen impeachment. There is no excuse for this behavior, but the Resistance justifies it as a required response to Trump, and the media gives the Resistance a pass.

What makes this behavior particularly despicable is that the leaders of the Resistance know better. They know politics; it is their daily bread and butter. They know their history, they know their Constitution, and they know their facts. And yet they are willing to twist and distort the truth, and ignore the rules, in order to benefit.

It's that mentality that differentiates the Resistance from prior political movements. America has had a lot of presidential elections, and each one has produced a losing side. Traditionally, the vanquished spend the ensuing years regrouping, opposing, and coming up with a better message. The Resistance from the start was instead about delegitimizing Trump, mobilizing the machinery of the government against him, and using any other means available to void the results of 2016. That zero-sum mentality all but guaranteed that the Resistance would immediately start taking out some of America's norms and institutions.

CHAPTER 2

ABOUT THAT AUTOCRAT

It's a scary thing when a president rules by executive order, ignores the law, threatens the fifty states, trains the federal bureaucracy on political opponents, and politicizes justice. And indeed, that Barack Obama dude was one scary president.

Donald Trump, not so much.

The most consistent and aggressive criticism of Trump is that he is a threat to American democracy—a budding autocrat who is destroying our most basic values and institutions. "Will American Democracy Survive Trump?" asked David Frum in *The Atlantic*. "America Is Slouching Toward Autocracy," warned the *Washington Post*'s E. J. Dionne. "2018: The Year of the Autocrat," declared the *Guardian* newspaper, lumping Trump in its lead paragraph along with Russia's Vladimir Putin and China's Xi Jinping.

Hitler, Stalin, Mao, King George, Genghis Khan, Kim Jong-un—Trump has been compared to them all. The more chilling predictions were, of course, always absurd. No, Trump never mobilized his own junta ("The Creeping Militarization of Donald Trump's Cabinet"—*Time*, December 2016). The 2018 midterm election came and went and saw Nancy Pelosi elected as Democratic House Speaker; Trump didn't send the Secret Service to steal her gavel. No, Trump has not brought on World War III ("How Trump Could Trigger Armageddon with a

Tweet"—*Wired*, September 2018). And no, Trump is not going to crown himself permanent leader ("Could Donald Trump Refuse to Leave Office When His Presidency Is Up?"—*New Statesman*, March 2018). He may inflict upon the nation an epic good-bye tour, but that's hardly a crime. See Bill Clinton.

The claims that have gained the most currency instead center on Trump's supposed abuses of power or his annihilation of democratic institutions. Before he was even inaugurated, Trump haters warned that he'd rule through fiat, abolish or neuter the courts, overrule Congress, mobilize the Justice Department against his enemies, shut down the press, and spy on his political enemies. Any number of these are felonies and impeachable offenses, and they are serious charges to lodge against a man who had yet to even measure curtains for the Oval Office.

They got away with the accusations partly because of Trump's style. The 45th president has no real filter. A lot of Americans, sick of the usual political spin and polish, admire him for it. Brainstorming is also valued in the business world, where Trump spent most of his adult life. CEOs throw out big, grand ideas, then wait for advisers to explain why a proposal won't work. But it's far riskier behavior for politicians, whose words and ideas are measured against highly complex law or policy. And Trump's think-out-loud statements are rarely vetted for legality, practicality, or conventionality.

Trump the candidate was particularly prone to produce spur-of-the-moment proposals, giving his opponents their opening to start the "autocrat" meme. An excellent example were his musings on foreign Muslims entering the country. In response to the 2015 San Bernardino shooting—in which two radicalized Muslims killed fourteen people—Trump called for "a total and complete shutdown of Muslims entering the United States until our country's representatives can figure out what the hell is going on." In a subsequent interview, Trump said this might require customs agents and border guards to ask every entrant about their religion—since such information isn't on passports.

He also said that the details "would have to be worked out"—acknowledging these were just thoughts. And in May 2016 he again noted the ban was "just a suggestion." According to former New York Mayor Rudy Giuliani, Trump early on asked advisers to look into "the right way to do it legally." By June he had explained the ban would apply geographically—not religiously—and only to countries with a "proven history of terrorism against the United States." And the final iteration of his travel ban—a presidential proclamation that suspended entry of certain citizens from a handful of terrorist-tied countries—was ruled constitutional by the Supreme Court.

But the damage was done. From the moment the candidate uttered his first thoughts through to the Supreme Court ruling, the ban was spun as a straight-up, discriminatory attack on the Muslim religion. The haters completely ignored Trump's terrorism argument. The ban was equated—despite wildly differing scenarios—to America's internment of Japanese Americans during World War II. The press warned that Trump would soon strip even Muslim-Americans of their rights. Years on, of course, this has not happened.

Or take the case of Gonzalo Curiel, the federal judge who in 2016 oversaw a class action suit against Trump University. Trump felt the judge's rulings were unfair and took to lambasting Curiel, even at one point suggesting the "Mexican" Curiel was biased against Trump because of his plans to build a wall. (Curiel was born in Indiana.)

The roasting of federal judges is hardly new. President Barack Obama slammed the Supreme Court over its Citizens United decision during his 2010 State of the Union Address. Republicans smacked around Chief Justice John Roberts for upholding Obamacare. But Trump's particularly pointed criticism allowed haters to spin his words as an unprecedented attack on an "independent judiciary" and proof that a President Trump would trample the Constitution's separation of powers. "Trump's personal, racially tinged attacks on federal judge alarm legal experts," explained the *Washington Post* on June 1, 2016. The article admitted that politicians criticize judges, but nonetheless insisted (with no real evidence) that Trump's attack was somehow terrifyingly different. His "vendetta signals a remarkable disregard for judicial independence" and carried "constitutional implications" if he won the election. But yet again, years into the Trump presidency, he has yet to disobey a single judicial order.

And, of course, nothing has dogged President Trump more than his impromptu remarks to Jim Comey about the FBI director's Russia probe, which the haters would ultimately use to initiate an entire special counsel probe into the Trump campaign, which dragged on for years. Much more on that later.

No question, Trump is impromptu. And no question he has changed the nature of the office of the presidency—in particularly disconcerting ways. He can be rude and brazen. Even his supporters sometimes wish someone would take away his phone. He's not too fussed with facts or consistency, which allows the press to pounce on his "lies." All these traits are among the reasons an October 2018 *Wall Street Journal*–NBC poll found that while nearly 44 percent of voters approved of his policies, nearly half of those people disliked him personally.

This is nonetheless personal behavior, limited to one of the more unusual figures to ever hold the U.S. presidency. At some point, Trump will leave office (yes, he will leave), and America will once again get a polished and polite (if potentially boring by comparison) president again. So the question becomes: Where will be the structural damage? Words are not the same as actions. The deceit the Trump haters have practiced all along has been to claim that Trump's mannerisms will result in the destruction of law, institutions, and democracy. There is no real evidence.

Quite the opposite. Any fair appraisal of the Trump administration will conclude that it has proven one of the more rule-bound and principled in modern history, at least in terms of the actual running of government. This fidelity to law and rules is, in fact, among the top reasons Trump voters so passionately support him. And it is why those same voters have such searing distrust of a media that constantly suggests otherwise.

Nor should this law-and-order reality come as a surprise to anyone willing to suspend the hysterics. The craziest predictions, that Trump would destroy democracy, were never realistic— if only because of structural safeguards. The Founding Fathers were highly aware that men are mere mortals. They'd risked their lives to get out from under a tyrant and specifically designed the Constitution and its checks and balances to guard against another. That Trump junta? Good luck when war powers are divided be-tween the executive and the legislative branches. Trump stripping entire classes of citizens of basic freedoms? The Supreme Court would knock that down in a nanosecond. Trump brazenly refus-ing to abide by such a Supreme Court order? Even a Republican Congress would move to impeach.

There's also the obvious point that Trump isn't unhinged, as the haters claim. The 45th president tends to respond to situa-tions with gut reactions. And because he makes himself readily accessible to the press, the world sometimes gets these raw, daily, often hourly, thoughts. But the record shows that Trump rarely demands action on unformed ideas. He reacts—then seeks coun-sel. That might be the opposite order of most presidents, but it still ends the country up at the same place—with considered, legal policies.

The travel ban is an example, but there are plenty of others. Trump once suggested he'd round up and deport every illegal im-migrant; he never did, in light of the overwhelming logistics and legal barriers to such an enormous operation. Angry over unfair press coverage in the campaign, Trump vowed that were he to win, he'd overhaul "libel laws so when they write purposely negative and horrible and false articles, we can sue them and win lots of money." He was at some point advised that there are no federal libel laws—they are issued by states—and nothing happened.

To the extent Trump has stretched the boundaries of presidential authority, it's generally been in keeping with prior presidential stretches. That includes his August 2017 pardon of the controversial Arizona Sheriff Joe Arpaio. A federal judge had held Arpaio in criminal contempt for flouting a court order governing his detention of illegal immigrants. The pardon was controversial even among conservatives. The Obama Justice Department had waged a relentless campaign against Arpaio, which many Trump supporters had viewed as unfair and political. They applauded Trump's intervention. Others wished Trump hadn't rewarded an official for ignoring a court and the law, and that Trump hadn't short-circuited the process by pardoning Arpaio before he'd been sentenced.

Nonetheless, a president's power to pardon is among the most awesome the Constitution grants, and Trump was within his legal rights to issue the Arpaio pardon. Moreover, name a president who hasn't issued a controversial pardon or commutation. President Clinton on his last day in office pardoned an international fugitive, Marc Rich, whose wife just happened to be a big Clinton donor. Obama commuted the sentences of both Chelsea Manning (who stole and dispersed American state secrets) and Oscar López Rivera, a violent Puerto Rican terrorist. Gerald Ford, of course, pardoned Nixon.

Yet despite all this, the press and Trump haters wrapped themselves into pretzel shapes to suggest the Arpaio pardon was unique and, worse, potentially criminal. "Why Trump's Pardon of Arpaio Follows Law, Yet Challenges It," wrote the *New York Times*. Its author, Adam Liptak, in the first paragraph editorialized that the pardon "concerned a crime" that was "particularly ill-suited to clemency" and "was not the product of the care and deliberation that have informed pardons by other presidents."

Whatever. "Arpaio Pardon Flouts Constitution, Ex–White House Officials Say," blared the *Guardian*, in a piece that offered no such evidence, even as it claimed Trump was "testing" his powers, gearing up to later pardon any of his people found guilty of Russia collusion.

One of the other big stretches of Trump's executive power came in February 2019, when he declared a national emergency at the southern border and used that as a reason to redirect funds to his planned wall. It came at the tail end of a grinding, two-month battle with Congress over border funds that resulted in the longest government shutdown in history. The spending bill Trump ultimately signed to reopen the government didn't include all the money he wanted for border security. So he invoked the National Emergencies Act of 1976, which allowed him to reroute up to $3.6 billion from other military construction projects to the wall.

Conservatives again were divided. Congressional critics—in particular military appropriators—were miffed that Trump was swiping funds that might otherwise go to their projects. Some constitutionalists decried the declaration as an assault on Congress's power over the purse. Yet others worried about the precedent Trump was setting. What was to stop a future Democratic president from declaring a national emergency over climate change or school shootings? These Republican detractors were, of course, joined by the entirety of the Democratic Congress and the press, which labeled the moment a "manufactured crisis" and an assault on the Constitution. "This is plainly a power grab by a disappointed president, who has gone outside the bounds of the law," declared congressional leaders Chuck Schumer and Nancy Pelosi in a joint statement. "Donald Trump's Emergency Declaration Is an Attack on Democracy," ran an opinion headline in *USA Today*, in which the author, Chris Truax, proclaimed that Trump was ruling "by decree."

And yet even a number of Republicans who were uneasy with

Trump's move admitted the legal question was hardly cut-and-dried. The National Emergencies Act is broad, and presidents have invoked it some sixty times, for all manner of crises. Some prior presidents had indeed used it to spend money that Congress hadn't approved—including after 9/11, when George W. Bush used emergency powers to ignore defense appropriations. A few commentators noted that Congress had chosen a weird time to suddenly get worried about the NEA. "Of the 59 national emergencies declared by presidents since 1979, more than half remain in effect today," wrote conservative columnist Edward Morrissey in *The Week*, pointing out that Congress has failed to revoke a single one. "It's going to be tough for Congress to argue in court that it's concerned about its constitutional privilege after decades of ignoring it."

And then there was the not-small question of whether the mess at the border did in fact count as . . . an emergency. Nebraska Senator Ben Sasse, one of Trump's most relentless GOP critics, ultimately voted to uphold the emergency declaration. Why? "We have an obvious crisis at the border—everyone who takes an honest look at the spiking drug and human trafficking numbers knows this," he said. Sasse reminded everyone that he and other constitutional conservatives had long worked to reform the NEA, which he decried as "overly broad" and ceding too much congressional "power" to the president. But precisely because nobody had reformed it, Sasse noted, "the President has a legal path."

The bigger point is that Trump's declaration was an uncharted use of executive power, not an assault on democracy. And the orderly process of resolving that legal question is proceeding per usual. Within days of the declaration, advocacy groups ranging from Public Citizen to the ACLU to the Center for Biological Diversity had readied or filed lawsuits challenging it. A coalition of sixteen states sued. The Democratic House sued (in a suit a federal judge threw out in June 2019 for lack of standing). The other claims are currently working through the courts, and at some point the country will have an answer on the limits of national emergency declarations. And the republic will continue to stand.

* * *

Finally, there is this glaringly obvious point: Trump and his team have no interest in breaking the law or wrecking institutions or undermining democracy. Quite the opposite. One of candidate Trump's campaign promises was an end to big, lawless government. That pledge was central to his election, coming as it did at a time when Americans—and conservatives in particular—had grown acutely concerned about presidential excesses.

All thanks to Barack Obama, who proved to be the most lawless and overreaching president in modern history. Obama's legislative achievements were almost entirely confined to his first two years in office, when a Democratic Senate and House provided to him his stimulus package, Obamacare, and Dodd-Frank financial regulation. But the 2010 Republican House takeover put an end to the free legislative pass. And rather than compromise or work with Republicans, Obama turned to executive power. "Where they won't act, I will," he vowed in 2011. "Wherever and whenever" he would "take steps without legislation."

The Constitution makes clear that Congress is supposed to make the laws. Obama made them himself. When Congress refused to provide him climate legislation, he directed his Environmental Protection Agency to do the same by regulatory fiat. When Congress wouldn't give him wetlands legislation, he directed the EPA to create the sweeping Waters of the United States rule—giving the federal government authority over every mud puddle in the country.

And in addition to the dubious legality of these rules there was their extraordinary cost, a flagrant government "taking"— as it were—from American companies and workers. According to George Washington University's Regulatory Studies Center, the Obama administration ultimately finalized an astonishing 490 "major" rules—defined as those that each inflict a cost of $100 million or more on the economy. Bill Clinton, by comparison, only mustered 361 over his own two terms. Even the *New York Times* acknowledged Obama's legacy was defined by "bureaucratic bulldozing rather than legislative transparency."

Obama was even more obnoxious with his use of executive orders. In March 2011, in response to calls that he unilaterally change immigration law, Obama said, "With respect to the notion that I can just suspend deportation through executive order, that's just not the case." Two months later he again acknowledged that he couldn't "bypass Congress and change the law myself." He explained: "That's not how a democracy works."

Yet when democracy didn't work out the way he liked, he did just that. In 2012 he issued his Deferred Action for Childhood Arrivals order, giving quasi-legal status to some 700,000 illegal aliens who were brought to the country as minors. In 2014 he issued an even broader order (DAPA), which provided administrative amnesty to millions more illegal immigrants. The second order was so howlingly extralegal that a federal judge issued an injunction before it was ever allowed to go into effect, the Fifth Circuit Court of Appeals upheld that injunction, and the Supreme Court maintained that ruling. DAPA never saw the light of day.

And when Obama didn't like laws that were on the books— including his own—his administration just changed them. In a January 2016 article in *Forbes*, Galen Institute President Grace-Marie Turner noted that Obamacare had been changed seventy significant times since its enactment in 2010. Some twenty-four of the changes were passed by Congress; another three were made by the Supreme Court. But many of the others the Obama administration imposed unilaterally, "without legal authority."

The 44th president also showed a blatant contempt for other

parts of the Constitution. In 2012, angry that Republicans were blocking some of his nominees, Obama unilaterally declared the Senate in recess. He then used his power of recess appointment to install three pro-union nominees to the National Labor Relations Board. The move was so obviously unconstitutional that all nine members of the Supreme Court unanimously rebuked the president in 2014. "The Senate is in session when it says it is," wrote liberal Justice Stephen Breyer. Yet Obama still got away with lawlessness, given that the Court was not brave enough to also strike down the hundreds of decisions that an unconstitutional NLRB majority had issued in the intervening time.

His agencies engaged in blatant power grabs and coercion, riding roughshod over states and federalism. They repeatedly used the threat of withholding federal funds to force policies onto the states. Obama Medicaid officials in 2015, for instance, threatened to cancel Medicaid funding for Florida unless it agreed to expand Obamacare. They also usurped traditional state power. The EPA in 2014 issued an unprecedented "pre emptive" veto of the Pebble Mine project in Alaska, denying the company, the state, and the Army Corps of Engineers the right to go through the usual permitting process. The veto put every state on notice that the EPA would now be the first, and only, arbiter of future development projects. Obama's land agencies—the EPA, the Bureau of Land Management, the National Park Service, the U.S. Forest Service—were so overbearing and punitive that they sparked a nascent new Sagebrush rebellion. The anger among Western landowners resulted at one point in the 2016 armed standoff between ranchers and the federal government at Oregon's Malheur National Wildlife Refuge.

Obama's IRS targeted political opponents. At urging from congressional Democrats, outside liberal groups, and the president himself, IRS official Lois Lerner and her nonprofit division threatened and abused hundreds of conservative Tea Party nonprofits that applied for tax-exempt status. The IRS's actions had the effect of silencing tens of thousands of conservative voices during both the 2010 midterms and the 2012 presidential election.

Agency heads routinely evaded federal transparency laws, to hide their doings from the public. Appointees and bureaucrats conducted business on private e-mail accounts or set up secondary, alias government accounts under fictitious names, making their correspondence harder to dig up with Freedom of Information Act requests. (Former EPA head Lisa Jackson used the nom de plume "Richard Windsor.") And let's not even get into former Secretary of State Hillary Clinton's private server, which gave her the power to unilaterally decide what any taxpayers would ever see of her work product.

Obama's Justice Department was a menace, routinely using its awesome powers to bully unpopular targets into settlements and payouts—financial institutions, oil companies, mining firms. DOJ diverted settlement money into a slush fund that it redistributed to favorite liberal interest groups. It, and other federal agencies, took to issuing "guidance" documents, extralegal rulings that allowed the administration to avoid the official rulemaking process. And the DOJ ran roughshod over constitutional protections for religious liberty and free speech.

Throughout, Obama continued to appoint liberal judges who had thoroughly "evolving" views of the Constitution and who could be trusted to wink and nod at, and legally justify, these overreaching, arrogant power grabs.

All of this makes the incessant allegation and emotion over the "lawless" Trump something close to hilarious. A politicized Justice Department? Check, under Obama. Ruling by decree? Did that, under Obama. Blatant disregard for checks and balances? Been there, under Obama. Changing laws at will? Hello, Obama.

This was the political moment Trump stepped into in late 2015, and even his initial presidential announcement speech—at the foot of that escalator—took aim at Obama's "illegal executive" immigration order. In February 2016 at a town hall in South Carolina, Trump highlighted how Obama used executive orders in the place of actual legislation, and he derided the practice. "This country wasn't based on executive orders," Trump said. "It's a basic disaster."

The theme of lawless government was central to the entire Republican primary and was further heightened in the final months—as the race came down to a duel between Trump and Ted Cruz. The Texas senator had blasted Obama's unchecked behavior over the years and made his promise to run as a "constitutional" conservative central to his campaign. Trump never embraced that label—indeed he rarely even today references the Constitution. But as the primary waged on, he put ever greater emphasis on the ideas behind that notion of conservatism. He promised to lower taxes, slash regulation, pull the United States out of extralegal agreements like the Paris Climate Accord, crack down on lobbyists and corporate welfare, and get rid of waste and fraud in government. And then there was his novel decision in May 2016 to release a list of potential Supreme Court nominees, from which he would choose a replacement for Antonin Scalia, who had died several months earlier. Trump's list was an all-star inventory of the brightest conservative legal minds in the country and represented, he said, the "constitutional principles" he valued. This vow—to stock the federal judiciary with judges committed to the rule of law, the separation of powers, and the Constitution—reassured millions of conservative voters and arguably won Trump the election.

Upon winning, Trump also immediately stocked his administration with the leading lights of this new constitutionalist-conservative movement. Many of these figures took jobs out of an edgy excitement that Trump really was a different kind of leader—and he intended to let them rein in government.

They included people like Don McGahn, who for two years served as Trump's general counsel. McGahn had spent years as a federal election commissioner struggling to rein in an out-of-control FEC bureaucracy that routinely sidestepped the appointed leaders. Putting government back in its box had become his mission in life. Or there was former South Carolina Representative Mick Mulvaney, whom Trump installed at the head of the Office of Management and Budget. Mulvaney was a founding member of the House Freedom Caucus, allied closely to the Tea Party movement, and passionately committed to reducing the size and scope of government. Scott Pruitt, the Oklahoma attorney general who had repeatedly sued the Obama administration for its unconstitutional acts, went to the EPA. Pruitt stated his intention to return the agency to its "statutorily-defined" mission, and to renew cooperation with the states. The federal Interior Department got as its head Montana Representative Ryan Zinke, a Westerner determined to once again put public lands to work for Americans, rather than cater to the whims of green groups. Elaine Chao, who had proven one of George W. Bush's most aggressive reformers as secretary of labor, returned to impose the same overhaul mentality to the Trump Transportation Department. And with all these big names came an army of like-minded constitutional conservatives, serving in other vital appointed positions in the Trump government.

Trump let this crew loose, and they didn't waste a millisecond. One year into the administration, *Politico* ran a piece headlined: "138 Things Trump Did This Year While You Weren't Looking." (A better headline would have been, "138 Things Trump Did That We Failed to Tell You About, Because We Were Too Obsessed with Russia," but at least *Politico* got there in the end.) The article, with a certain amount of surprised concern, noted the obvious: "Steadily, and almost totally separately from Trump's speeches and tweetstorms, his administration has been ushering in a new conservative era of government."

These legions of conservative advisers act as a natural brake on some of Trump's off-the-cuff proposals, even as they work to meld his more unconventional approach to the law. Trump views his job as pushing the boundaries of government-as-usual; they view theirs as making sure this conforms with statutes and regulations. A great example was the 2018–2019 government shutdown. Most administrations try to make shutdowns as politically painful as possible, so as to get Congress to roll. They furlough workers, close national parks, withhold money from vital programs.

Trump wanted to do the exact opposite; he wanted to hold out as long as possible, to force Democrats to meet his border security demands. This had never been done before, and it required an entire team of OMB employees, led by General Counsel Mark Paoletta, working day and night, to figure out how to legally continue paying some government bills without running afoul of federal laws. Their work was among the reasons that the Coast Guard got checks, Americans continued to get food stamps, and the IRS kept processing tax returns. Was the shutdown a good idea? Maybe not. Was it legal? Absolutely.

Those advisers also helped Trump bring to a screeching halt the Obama pen-and-phone method. It's not that Trump didn't issue executive orders—he did. Amusingly, the press used his early embrace of them as yet further, alarmed evidence that he was governing as a tyrant. Trump is about to sign "a record number of executive orders in his first 100 days," blared the Associated Press, noting that he was "turning to a presidential tool he once derided."

What the critics didn't note is that Trump's orders were almost exclusively focused on *rolling back* government, keeping it in line. One order imposed a five-year ban on executive branch employees from federal lobbying. One implemented a novel regulatory "budget," ordering every department and agency to slash two regulations for every new one proposed. Regulation spending could also not, overall, exceed $0. One ordered a review of financial regulations, with the goal of ending government bailouts. One expedited federal environmental reviews for high-priority infrastructure projects. One ordered the EPA to get rid of the horrific Waters of the United States rule. One ordered Mulvaney at OMB to produce a plan to reorganize governmental functions and eliminate unnecessary agencies. One gave agencies the authority to issue waivers and exemptions of Obamacare, given its increasingly crushing costs. All this was the opposite of Obama's use of executive orders to extralegally create more government.

Trump has overseen the most dramatic reduction in the size of federal government of any president in the modern era. He allied with Republicans to employ the Congressional Review Act, a previously little-used legislative tool for overriding bad regulation. The act allows simple majorities of the House and the Senate to strike down any rule written in the past sixty legislative days. Obama had engaged in a flurry of midnight regulation, working to force through as much government expansion as possible in the waning months of his administration. All of those rules were subject to the CRA, and between Trump and the Republican Congress, they struck down sixteen major Obama regulations—including rules designed to shut down mining, oil, and gas operations; strangle payday lending; and squelch hunting in Alaska.

And these victories paled by comparison to the Trump administration's internal deregulation. By December 2017—less than a year into his presidency—the Trump team announced it had canceled or delayed more than 1,500 planned Obama regulations—eliminating 22 rules for every proposed 1. In October 2018, it issued a new report showing that even in its second year, it had hit a 12-to-1 deregulatory ratio, saving the economy $23 billion in costs.

The national government compiles all its rules and regulations into what's called the Federal Register, and for decades that book has consistently grown, usually year-on-year. Obama finished his final 2016 calendar year with an all-time Federal Register record of 95,894 pages. A year later, on December 29, 2017, the first year of Trump, the Federal Register concluded at 61,308 pages. It was the lowest count since 1993, Bill Clinton's first year in office. By the end of 2018, an analysis by the Competitive Enterprise Institute showed that Trump had issued the fewest number of regulations in recorded history in his first two years of office. Tyrants don't get rid of rules; they pile them on.

The press has also missed the extraordinary efforts the Trump administration has taken to make it harder for bureaucracies *in the future* to restart the rule-making engine. McGahn told me that when he took the top Trump legal job, he brought with it two overriding goals—both aimed at neutering an increasingly lawless federal workforce. The first was to confirm into every department and agency a general counsel and team of lawyers who in addition to deregulation have also put in place rules that should make it harder for current and future bureaucrats to overstep their statutory boundaries.

McGahn's other achievement was to ensure Trump's remake of the federal judiciary also put new focus on bureaucrats. McGahn didn't just want stellar conservative judges; he had other filters. He wanted young judges: people in their forties and fifties who'd be able to serve for decades on the federal bench. He also wanted judges with a deep understanding of administrative law and the separation of powers. In the 1980s, conservatives obsessed about judicial litmus tests like abortion. But as the years rolled on, and federal bureaucrats grew more powerful, conservative organizations such as the Federalist Society became equally obsessed with judges who understood the unique challenge of our big-government times. They began to focus on the Supreme Court's 35-year-old Chevron precedent, which holds that courts should defer to federal bureaucrats' interpretation of law. The Constitution, they note, tasks a confirmed and accountable judiciary with settling law—not nameless, faceless worker bees.

McGahn hasn't received enough credit for his work with the Federalist Society to come up with a list of judges uniquely qualified to take on big government. He and Federalist Society executive vice president Leonard Leo, along with Senate majority leader

Mitch McConnell, have been rightly praised for the sheer number and quality of constitutionally sound judges they placed. By December 2019, McConnell had successfully voted through 187 judges, including fifty appeals court judges and two Supreme Court justices. The circuit court and high court numbers were particularly consequential. Trump in three years successfully filled nearly 25 percent of all appeals court judgeships with his picks. As for the Supreme Court, his appointments of conservatives Neil Gorsuch and Brett Kavanaugh guaranteed a truly conservative majority for the first time in decades.

But McGahn's bigger victory was in the type of conservative judges. A significant number of Trump's appeals court picks were in their forties, guaranteeing decades of service on those crucial courts that are just one step below the Supremes. And these younger judges in particular had cut their teeth in a new era of big-government legal battles. Both Gorsuch and Kavanaugh were rightly feted upon nomination as brilliant jurists with outstanding intellects, devoted to deciding cases based on the clear language of the law. Less noticed is that both men had been vocal as lower-court judges about challenging Chevron, and the wisdom of letting bureaucrats run the show. In a 2016 opinion, while still serving as a Tenth Circuit court judge, Gorsuch derided Chevron as "judge-made doctrine for the abdication of the judicial duty."

Trump put in place dozens of judges who share an overriding fidelity to the law and an interest in restraining oppressive government. "Autocrats" are all about growing their power; they don't embrace smaller government. They don't sign orders and hire people focused on restraining the scope of federal power. And "autocrats" don't strengthen a rival branch (the judiciary) with a new generation of judges who exist to keep the executive branch in line. The entire Trump-as-tyrant narrative is nonsensical.

Even the haters know this. In his "America Is Slouching Toward Autocracy" piece, the *Washington Post*'s E. J. Dionne warned voters not to trust that "checks, balances and other circuit-breakers" would stop Trump from "subverting basic freedoms." Yet in the entirety of a piece devoted to Trump's budding "autocracy," here was the totality of Dionne's complaint: Trump is too mean to the press and his opponents while too nice to foreign despots; Trump failed to release his taxes; Trump tells falsehoods; Trump fired Jim Comey. Dionne offers not one example of how any of this had destroyed democracy or government institutions. A lot of Americans (including, secretly, Democrats), in fact, agree that the canning of Jim Comey was the best thing that ever happened to the FBI.

Trump's efforts to rein in corrosive government is, if anything, a huge reason why so many former Never Trumpers have become more open to his presidency. In a March 2018 column in *Politico* titled "The Never Trump Delusion," Rich Lowry—editor of the same *National Review* that had two years earlier run an issue against Trump—lightly scolded his "friends" on the Never Trump right who remain in "denial." "A realistic attitude to Trump involves acknowledging both his flaws and how he usefully points the way beyond a tired Reagan nostalgia. By all means, criticize when he's wrong, but don't pretend he's just going away, or that he's a wild outlier in the contemporary GOP," he wrote.

Some former Never Trumpers have, in fact, become enormous defenders of the 45th president. Why? Partly because of Trump's conservative achievements. More important, because they have become alarmed by the damage they *do* see happening to U.S. institutions and democracy: the damage inflicted by Trump haters in their zeal to bring down the president.

While the Resistance traffics in false equivalence and meritless accusations against Trump, the evidence of their own wreckage is on full display. The Justice Department, the FBI, the federal judiciary, the bureaucracy, the Senate—all are littered with the debris of their scorched-earth campaigns against the president. And it could be a long time—if ever—before the country recovers.

CHAPTER 3

J. EDGAR COMEY

How do you wreck an FBI? In the course of eighteen months, the Federal Bureau of Investigation went from one of the more trusted law enforcement institutions on the planet to a hollowed-out shell, its morale and reputation in shambles.

Director Jim Comey: fired for insubordination. Deputy Director Andy McCabe: terminated for lying to investigators. Senior Counterintelligence Agent Peter Strzok: dismissed for partisan bias. General Counsel James Baker: reassigned and then out on resignation—part of a federal criminal leak investigation. These were just the highlights among a dozen senior FBI leaders who were fired or faded away. They included chief of staff James Rybicki; lawyer Lisa Page; the assistant director of the Counterintelligence Division, Bill Priestap; the head of the National Security Division, Michael Steinbach; the FBI's top congressional liaison, Greg Brower; and the assistant director for public affairs (and 33-year FBI veteran), Michael Kortan.

Support for the FBI meanwhile cratered—at least among the half of the country that leans right. These are the voters who most traditionally support law enforcement, but now view this vital American institution with skepticism or disdain. A May 2018 Rasmussen poll found that a full 72% of likely Republican voters thought it likely that senior federal law enforcement officials broke the law in an effort to prevent Trump from winning the presidency.

The McCourtney Institute for Democracy at Penn State in February 2018 asked Americans: "How much of the time do you think you can trust the FBI to do what is right?" A dismal 39% of Republicans felt the FBI could be trusted "most of the time" or "just about always," and only 45% of independents. A full 54% of Republicans felt FBI agents were "biased against President Trump and his agenda." Among Republicans aged forty-five or older—which McCourtney noted is "a generation . . . socialized to see the FBI as the epitome of American law enforcement"—the fear of FBI bias soared to 60%. The Institute noted that these findings of mass disillusionment were of "concern," given that "in the past, the Justice Department and FBI have generally been recognized as the most independent of the cabinet agencies."

Trump opponents (including the McCourtney Institute) try to lay all this off on Trump himself. His relentless attacks on the FBI and former Special Counsel Bob Mueller, they say, have inspired Americans to view law enforcement in partisan terms. In fact, politicians who unfairly attack venerable American institutions usually get nothing but blowback. The only times their complaints find traction are when Americans understand that the institution deserves the criticism.

And "wrong" doesn't even adequately summarize the FBI's behavior in 2016–17. Its leaders broke every rule, and also a sacred public trust.

* * *

Was it "partisanship" that drove Comey and his band of rogues to try to take down a presidency? There isn't much evidence of that—at least not in the technical sense of that word. To be a "partisan" is to be a fervent supporter of a party or a person. It seems unlikely that Comey and Co.—many of whom were, in fact, Republicans—were moved to act because they disagreed with GOP tax and health care policies or were enamored with Hillary Clinton.

Given what we know now, it's far more likely that Jim Comey came down with one of the first—if at-that-time-undiagnosed—cases of Trump Derangement Syndrome. In hindsight, it's clear the degree to which the FBI director *from the start* treated President Trump as a threat to law enforcement and the country. He helped engineer the public exposure of scandalous oppo-research on the campaign. He memorialized his conversations with the new commander in chief, with an eye to later leaking his one-sided judgments. He worked to entrap members of the new administration like former National Security Advisor Michael Flynn. These aren't the actions of a professional FBI director who is neutral as to the country's choice of a president.

After he was fired, Comey also made clear publicly the depth of his loathing for Trump—which surely existed from the start. In his book, *A Higher Loyalty*, he compares Trump to a Mafia boss, likens his presidency to a "forest fire," accuses him of being "untethered to truth." He has slammed Trump for lying about the Bureau "constantly," and called on all Americans to mobilize to vote him out in 2020. He uses every press appearance, every tweet, to deride the president of the United States. It's something nearing an obsession. The Obama CIA director, John Brennan, also unloaded on Trump after leaving office, accusing him of everything from "venality" to "moral turpitude" to "political corruption." These Comey and Brennan statements reflect remarkably visceral levels of hate—ones that could not have come about overnight. Text messages between Strzok and Page more likely reflect the general sentiment about Trump within the DOJ and CIA leadership in the run-up to the election. They refer to him as an "idiot," a "loathsome human," "pathetic," and a "do*che." At one point Page asks for reassurance that Trump is "not ever going to become president, right?" Strzok responds: "No. No he's not. We'll stop it."

Lots of Americans hated Trump. But Comey had two advantages over his fellow haters. The first: his own infamous self-regard. Over his decades in Washington, Comey had carefully cultivated a persona—that of the last guy in D.C. who believed in truth, justice, and the American way; the last guy willing to do the right thing. He'd dined out for years on his telling (and retelling and retelling) of the story of how as deputy attorney general he'd stood up to George W. Bush and Dick Cheney over one of their surveillance programs—threatening to quit (along with then–FBI Director Bob Mueller) if it did not end. As his book title—*A Higher Loyalty*—makes clear, at some point Comey began to believe his own baloney. Former Deputy Attorney General Rod Rosenstein would astutely note that Comey's problem was that he got in the business of judging "character" and "soul." But "speculating about souls is not a job for police and prosecutors," said Rosenstein. "Generally, we base our opinions on eyewitness testimony."

This arrogance fueled a second Comey quality: a disregard for the rules. His prosecutorial record shows that when Comey couldn't bring down his targets for the crimes of which they were accused, he'd twist the law or use abusive tactics to get them on a technicality. When Comey couldn't nail Martha Stewart for insider trading, he jailed her for "lying." When Comey couldn't indict banker Frank Quattrone on financial crimes, he concocted a farcical "obstruction of justice" charge—later tossed out by a court. And Comey and Mueller would waste millions of dollars and pervert investigative techniques as part of their botched (and incorrect) investigation of Steven Hatfill on anthrax charges. On June 23, 2013, as Obama was receiving accolades for his decision to name Comey the new FBI director, we at the *WSJ* ran an editorial reprising these lowlights of his career and offering a warning: "America already had an FBI director who thought he was accountable to no political master and ruined many lives. There's a building named after him in Washington, D.C., but one such director is more than enough."

It took only three years on that all-powerful FBI job for Comey to move beyond restraint. It was July 2016, when the FBI director jumped the Justice Department chain of command, and took it upon himself to decide and announce that there would be no charges against Hillary Clinton for mishandling classified information. The Justice Department inspector general would later describe Comey's decision to place himself above his bosses as rank "insubordination."

Enter Candidate Trump in the spring of 2016. He didn't know it, but he faced an FBI director who despised him and who believed himself above the rules that govern mere mortals. And just how many of those rules did the FBI break in the 2016 campaign year? Countless.

* * *

Let's start with a basic rule: The Department of Justice has strict guidelines about engaging in political activities. A 2012 memo issued by no less than Obama Attorney General Eric Holder reiterated these long-standing principles. Titled "Election Year Sensitivities," Mr. Holder reminded employees that while the department has a "strong interest" in the prosecution of crimes, it must be "particularly sensitive to safeguarding the Department's reputation for fairness, neutrality and nonpartisanship. Simply put, politics must play no role in the decisions of federal investigators or prosecutors regarding any investigations or criminal charges." While the memo did not mention it specifically, it also served as a reminder of the Justice Department's informal policy of avoiding DOJ action in the sixty days preceding an election.

By any standard, the Comey probes into Clinton and Trump blew these rules all to hell. The FBI arguably couldn't avoid looking into the Clinton server mess, given the inspector general of the intelligence community referred it to the Bureau in 2015, citing concerns that Clinton had mishandled classified information. Comey's team in fairness also sought to complete that investigation before the Democratic nomination convention in 2016. But Comey's decision to publicly chastise Clinton—putting the FBI in the position of morally judging a putative nominee for the presidency—and his subsequent decision to publicly reopen that Clinton investigation just before Election Day, broke all DOJ rules.

As for its handling of the Trump-Russia collusion case, the FBI's actions were "political" from Day One. And Day One—contrary to the FBI's telling—looks to be very early in 2016. It was late March 2016 when the Trump campaign announced its foreign policy advisory team. Trump was under fire for not having a brain trust, and the list included names few had ever heard before—among them a former investment banker named Carter Page and an energy consultant named George Papadopoulos. Days later, the Trump campaign announced it had brought on board veteran GOP strategist and lobbyist Paul Manafort, to help corral delegates.

The FBI's ears perked up. Both Page and Manafort had been on the Bureau's radar before. Page had worked for Merrill Lynch in Russia and in 2013 had been targeted by Russian intelligence for possible recruitment. But the FBI never accused Page of wrongdoing, and Page assisted with the FBI's efforts to take down the Russian agents. The FBI reportedly had also been looking at Manafort, who at one point worked on behalf of the Ukrainian ruling party.

This is the point at which the FBI first stepped off its rails. When the Bureau fears a political leader or campaign has a security risk, it has a standard protocol: It offers a defensive briefing. That's exactly what it did, for instance, in 2013, when it became alarmed that a staffer in Senator Dianne Feinstein's California office had been targeted by Chinese intelligence. Feinstein immediately got rid of the staffer and would later insist he never had access to any "sensitive information."

The FBI had even better reasons to offer a defensive briefing in

Trump's case. Page and Manafort had only just joined the campaign and had no real ties to the candidate. Page in particular was serving on an unpaid basis and in a role far removed from central decision making. The Trump campaign, while somewhat disorganized, also had two obvious advisers to whom the FBI could have taken its concerns. Both Chris Christie and Rudy Giuliani were former U.S. attorneys in the Department of Justice. Finally, the FBI—in light of those Justice Department guidelines to be "sensitive" to political matters—had good cause to handle the situation straightforwardly, to avoid any whiff that an incumbent administration was snooping on a political rival. Had it taken the simple briefing step, the nation might have been spared years of turmoil.

But not briefing Trump was just half of the bad decision. The other half was the Bureau's decision to instead brief Trump's political rivals—Democrats. According to congressional investigators, sometime in "late spring" FBI Director Comey told the principal members of the Obama White House National Security Council that the Bureau had eyes on Trump and Russia. We don't know the exact date, and we don't know exactly who attended. But the Obama principals would have included Obama himself, Susan Rice (national security advisor), James Clapper (director of national intelligence), John Brennan (CIA director), Loretta Lynch (attorney general), and a number of cabinet secretaries. Comey's decision to alert the nation's most senior Democratic political team to the FBI's interest in Trump-Russia ties was at best reckless, at worst calculated. Because one obvious question is whether Team Obama in turn whispered to the Clinton campaign—especially in light of the giant "coincidence" that came next.

* * *

Nobody should ever want the FBI working at the behest of, or on behalf of, a political campaign. Imagine if the Trump White House in early 2020 ordered the FBI to open a counterintelligence investigation into the leading Democratic contender for the White House. The press and the public would go bananas. And yet this is essentially what happened in 2016, albeit with a bit more sophistication. The FBI became an active or unwitting tool of the Clinton cabal.

It so happens that around the same time of this Comey briefing—also in "late spring"—the Clinton campaign and the Democratic National Committee hired Fusion GPS, an opposition-research firm, to investigate . . . Trump-Russia ties. The contract was officially signed by Perkins Coie, the law firm representing Clinton and the DNC. This allowed Democrats to hide from public view that they were retaining an oppo shop. Fusion was the creation of former *Wall Street Journal* reporters Glenn Simpson and Peter Fritsch, and in just a few years had developed a reputation for dumpster diving—mostly on behalf of Democrats.

Trump haters—including Comey—to this day spin the falsehood that it was Republicans who hired Fusion to look into Trump's Russia interactions. They do so because they know the truth—that the FBI aided Clinton against her political opponent—sounds as terrible as it is.

Here's what actually happened: The *Washington Free Beacon*, a conservative outlet funded by major Republican donor Paul Singer, commissioned Fusion to do broad opposition research on Trump. But as Trump neared the nomination in spring, the *Free Beacon* called off the dogs. Fusion then offered its services to Perkins Coie. Simpson acknowledged in 2017 Senate testimony that Fusion was not "totally focused on Russia at that time." But in "late spring" it suddenly was—around the same time the Obama White House learned about the FBI's interest in the Trump campaign.

Fusion then turned to one of the few men capable of pulling off what now ranks as the dirtiest political trick in modern U.S. history. Christopher Steele had spent some twenty years at Britain's MI6 intelligence service, including on the Russia desk. In 2009, he, like Simpson, found an easier way to cash in on "research." He set out his shingle as a private "intelligence" operator for hire. Steele in that capacity did work for England's Football Association that put him in touch with the FBI. That meant he had an "in" with the Bureau; Fusion used it.

Steele from June to December authored seventeen reports on the Trump campaign and Russia—the now infamous "dossier." It was an absurd collection of surreal allegations, many conveniently centered on Page and Manafort—the very men the FBI just happened to have in its sights. Several claimed that Page on a July 2016 trip to Moscow had secretly met with a Kremlin power player, who had offered the Trump campaign compromising Clinton material. He'd also, the dossier said, clandestinely met with the head of a Russian oil company, Rosneft, who offered Page the brokerage on 19 percent of that company in return for Trump lifting Russia sanctions. One report put Manafort at the center of a "well developed conspiracy" between the Trump campaign and Russia, in which Page served as an intermediary. Another said Page had "conceived and promoted" the idea of leaking stolen Democratic e-mails to WikiLeaks. South Carolina Representative Trey Gowdy would later quip that the entire dossier read like the *National Enquirer*.

Steele's most explosive report turned out to be his first, crafted in June, in which he claimed the Russians were already regularly feeding "intelligence" to the Trump campaign, and that they had compromising video of Trump performing "perverted sexual acts" while in a Moscow hotel room in 2013. Steele immediately called up his old U.S. law enforcement buddies, and delivered this bombshell accusation at a July 5 meeting in London with an FBI agent.

Give Steele and Fusion credit for cleverness. Normally, political campaigns have to "shop" their oppo-research to the media, and convince reporters of its accuracy. Fusion knew this was a dead end; nothing in the report was verified, as a Justice Department Inspector General report would later confirm. So Steele instead took the

Clinton oppo-research to the FBI and peddled it as "intelligence." And once the FBI took possession, Steele and Fusion were able to point the media to the Bureau and the investigation itself. The media never had to take responsibility for the veracity of the claims, and Fusion and the Clinton campaign still got their phony narrative.

What did the FBI immediately do with that information? We don't know. The Bureau has gone to huge lengths to hide its actions during July. But we know what it should have done. The FBI has rules requiring it to thoroughly vet its sources for motivation and credibility. Nothing about Steele's ludicrous tale passed a basic sniff test.

Consider the sheer absurdity of his 007 claims. At the time Steele put together his first dossier report, he had not been active in professional intelligence circles in seven years. Yet his report insisted it was informed by sources intimately connected to Putin—whose Kremlin is otherwise impenetrable. Steele was claiming to have unraveled the greatest political conspiracy in a generation, one that every other intelligence agency on the planet—possessing the most sophisticated spycraft tools available—had missed. And he was suggesting he'd done it in the space of a few weeks, using nothing more than his telephone.

Then there was the craziness of the information itself, which grew with each report and which suggested that everyone in the entire Kremlin was spilling their guts to him. This sudden flood of Russian information should have set off enormous FBI alarm bells. Early in his career, Steele worked under diplomatic cover as an MI6 agent in Moscow, and later under diplomatic cover in Paris. But that cover was blown in 1999, when a disaffected former MI6 agent publicly listed the names of 117 British spies. Steele, in other words, was known to the Russians.

In his private career, he'd also taken to sending reports on Russia and Ukraine to the U.S. State Department. Former Obama State Department official Jonathan Winer would in 2018 admit that he'd been friendly with Steele since 2009, and starting as early as 2013 had arranged for "more than 100 of Steele's reports" on Russia to be shared with his State colleagues. Were any Russians aware of Steele's relationships with U.S. actors in the FBI and State? The U.S. intelligence community by mid-2016 knew Russia was attempting to interfere in the U.S. election. Russians are famous for disinformation campaigns, and the FBI was in fact warned that the Steele information was a potential plant by an adversary. (More on Mueller's failure to investigate this in Chapter 6.)

Had the FBI done due diligence, it would have also discovered that Steele had links to Oleg Deripaska, a Russian oligarch with Kremlin ties. E-mails show that in 2016—separate from his work on the dossier—Steele was probing and pushing U.S. government contacts for information about a U.S. visa Deripaska wanted. Steele, on the one hand, was telling the FBI he wanted to help protect the U.S. against Russian influence. He was, on the other hand, tied to influential Russians. This certainly undermined his credibility.

The FBI might also have discovered that Steele's pals at Fusion were *also* tied up with Russians. Natalia Veselnitskaya, a Russian lawyer with Kremlin ties, was laboring in early 2016 to defend a Russian company against federal money-laundering charges. Fusion was hired, via a U.S. law firm, to dredge up negative information on the men who had helped bring to light that reported fraud.

This was the same Veselnitskaya who in June 2016 sought a meeting with Donald Trump Jr., Manafort, and Jared Kushner. She initially claimed to have dirt on the Clinton campaign, but when she showed up at Trump Tower, she instead wanted to talk about Russian sanctions. Veselnitskaya met with Simpson both before and after that Trump Tower event. Simpson denies any knowledge of that meeting and insists Fusion's work on the dossier was kept separate from its work for a Kremlin-linked attorney. But an FBI that did its homework on its sources would have had serious concerns about the integrity of the Fusion-Steele operation.

Then again, maybe the FBI did know all this and just ignored it. That would at least explain its decision to also ignore the clear evidence that Fusion and Steele were using the Bureau to grind a political axe. And helping out political actors is also a clear violation of FBI rules.

As the summer went on, Steele and his taskmasters engaged in a concerted pressure campaign to get the FBI to act, dumping their dossier with other government sources. Steele sat down for breakfast on July 30, 2016, with an old Justice Department buddy and associate attorney general, Bruce Ohr. It was a pretty clubby meal. Ohr's wife, Nellie, also worked for Fusion GPS, helping with the oppo-research against Trump. During the meeting with the Ohrs, Steele passed along his dossier information. Bruce Ohr immediately turned around and gave the oppo to the FBI's then–Deputy Director Andy McCabe as well as lawyer Lisa Page. In August, Ohr says, he took it to Peter Strzok, the Bureau's lead Trump-Russia investigator. And at some point he additionally briefed senior personnel in the Justice Department's Criminal Division. This helped ensure that by August, pretty much every FBI and DOJ leader involved in the Trump-Russia investigation was aware of the dossier.

Steele meanwhile went to his State Department friend, Winer, in the summer of 2016, and warned him about possible ties between Trump and Russians. By September, Winer had reviewed the dossier and passed a summary straight up to Secretary of State John Kerry. Winer admitted he also passed along Steele information to Sydney Blumenthal, a Hillary Clinton operator. And in October, Steele sat down to discuss his dossier with Deputy Assistant Secretary of State Kathleen Kavalec, who sent a memo to colleagues explaining that Steele was "keen to see this information come to light prior to November 8." Steele's political motives were clear.

And then there was FBI general counsel James Baker. At some point that fall, Mr. Baker's self-described "old friend" David Corn, a *Mother Jones* reporter, reached out. Corn, too, had a copy of the dossier to deliver to the FBI, which Baker later said he "assumed" Corn got from "Simpson, or someone acting on Simpson's behalf." In congressional testimony, Mr. Baker explained that the FBI *knew* Fusion was papering the FBI and the town with its opposition research. "My recollection is that [Corn] had part of the dossier, that we had other parts already, and that we got still other parts from other people," said Baker. He further admitted: "My understanding at the time was that Simpson was going around Washington giving this out to a lot of different people and trying to elevate its profile."

This was a clear political hit job, and if that wasn't already obvious to the FBI, Mr. Baker got another call in the fall, this one from an acquaintance named Michael Sussmann. He, too, was a Clinton-DNC lawyer at Perkins Coie and, oddly, wanted to meet in person. Baker made the phenomenally poor decision to directly sit down with a Clinton representative and accept by hand a further passel of allegations about Trump misdeeds. The general counsel admitted in congressional testimony that all this was way out of protocol: evidence does not normally flow through the FBI's general counsel. He acknowledged he was likely targeted by both Corn and Sussmann in their hopes that any information passed along from an FBI general counsel would automatically be taken seriously. He also implicitly admitted how inappropriate it was for the FBI's top lawyer to be accepting dirt from a political operative during the run-up to a presidential election. He said he was concerned about the Sussmann material "from the first instance," and that as "soon as" Sussmann left, he called FBI agents and "got rid of the material as quickly as I could."

Which gets to the ultimate reason the FBI should have run from the dossier: It came from the Clinton campaign, and the FBI knew it. Remember that DOJ memo from Holder stressing political sensitivities? The seasoned professionals at the FBI knew better. Heck, even the public understood how wrong it was to go down this road. In December 2017, a Harvard CAPS-Harris poll queried the public's view of the dossier. A full 58 percent of respondents agreed that if the dossier was funded by Clinton and Democrats, it could not be used by law enforcement.

This might explain why Comey purposely maintains a blasé attitude about the dossier to this day, claiming he can't really remember much about when he was briefed, never really knew exactly who funded it, etc. Such information, he testified, "didn't matter" in light of the fact that it came from a "reliable source."

Disingenuous, and likely untrue. Congressional testimony proves that the entirety of Comey's inner circle knew about the dossier's provenance, and well before the election. They never told their boss? When Bruce Ohr turned over the dossier in mid-summer to McCabe and Page, he did so with a warning. He testified that he told the senior leadership of the FBI that the Steele info was politically biased and unproven: "When I provided [the Steele information] to the FBI, I tried to be clear that this is source information," he testified. "I don't know how reliable it is. You're going to have to check it out and be aware. These guys were hired by somebody relating to—who's related to the Clinton campaign, and be aware." He also told the team that Steele was "desperate that Donald Trump not get elected."

Baker said that the FBI was aware of the dossier's provenance, and that it was playing with fire. He explained that one of the reasons he later took such a close interest in an October 2016 application to eavesdrop on Page was because "there were a range of issues with respect to the providence [sic] of this information and the relationship that we had with respect to Mr. Simpson and his credibility."

The FBI was getting beat over the head with signs it was being used and played. It closed its eyes and continued breaking rules.

* * *

The FBI leaders and agents who ran the 2016 probe have worked hard to suggest that they had an unlimited right to pursue the Trump campaign and that their actions were routine. In fact, the FBI has a huge manual—the *Domestic Investigations and Operations Guide*—that lays out strict rules and procedures. The guide includes entire sections on "privacy" and "civil liberties"; the need to use "least intrusive methods"; the importance of having honest "predications" for investigations; rules about "undercover operations" and "the monitoring of communications" and even the "acquisition of foreign intelligence information." Investigations are also normally run out of field offices, allowing FBI headquarters to act as a check on satellite behavior. Comey instead decided to run the Trump probe out of headquarters itself. And with no higher authority to stop them, he and his investigators threw the manual out the window.

In March 2016, a young and relatively inexperienced policy junkie named George Papadopoulos joined the Trump campaign as an unpaid adviser. Papadopoulos at the time was working for the London Centre of International Law Practice. About a month after joining the Trump team, Papadopoulos sat down in London with a person he'd met through work, Joseph Mifsud. Mifsud was a Maltese professor. He remains a mysterious figure, one that has seeming connections both to Russian academics and to Western intelligence officials. At their breakfast on April 26, 2016, Mifsud is said to have told Papadopoulos that the Russians had material on Clinton that could be damaging to her.

Only a few weeks later, Papadopoulos found himself having drinks with Alexander Downer, who was at that time Australia's top representative in the United Kingdom. It's still unclear why someone as high-ranking as Downer was meeting with such a minor Trump aide. Papadopoulos got to gossiping and passed along what he'd heard about the Russians and Clinton. More than two months after that, following news that the DNC had been hacked, Downer related to the U.S. government what he'd heard from Papadopoulos. A few days after *that,* July 31, 2016, the FBI opened its counterintelligence probe into Trump officials.

This is the "origin" story, the FBI's public explanation of how it came to spy on a presidential campaign. The FBI only leaked this version of events to its media scribes after it stood accused of using the dossier to launch its probe, and there are many reasons to doubt it is the whole truth. But even if you buy the Papadopoulos-launched-it-all claim, the FBI would be hard-pressed to argue that this one episode warranted a full-fledged counterintelligence investigation.

Papadopoulos, like Page, was largely peripheral to the campaign. He believed his task was to improve U.S.-Russia relations and spent time attempting to facilitate meetings between Trump officials and Russians—but uniformly struck out. Add to this that the FBI had no real evidence of wrongdoing. They had a game of telephone. A non-Russian professor repeated something to a third-tier campaign aide, who repeated it to a random diplomat, who repeated it to the FBI. On this basis, we get a probe of a presidential campaign?

And something clearly got lost in the repetition. The FBI, Mueller, and the media have steadfastly maintained that Papadopoulos mattered because Mifsud told him about "thousands of emails" pertaining to Clinton months before the DNC hack. This, they said, suggested that Mifsud had intimate knowledge of the Kremlin's efforts, before that hack became public. Yet the "thousands of emails" could just have easily been a reference to the e-mails Clinton had kept on (and then deleted from) her private server while she was secretary of state—e-mails that were the subject of rampant public speculation at that time.

Meanwhile, two former colleagues of Mifsud recently wrote a book, *The Faking of Russia-gate,* in which they claimed to have interviewed the now-hiding professor. They write that he stated "vehemently that he never told anything like this to George Papadopoulos." Papadopoulos, for his part, says he doesn't remember sharing any relevant information with Downer. And in an interview with *The Australian*, Downer was emphatic that Papadopoulos did not offer him any specifics. "He didn't say dirt, he said material that could be damaging to [Clinton]," said Mr. Downer. "He didn't say what it was." If this is true, the FBI was told only that Papadopoulos had heard the Russians had something on Hillary—no mention of e-mails. This would make their decision to launch an entire investigation even more absurd.

Also disconcerting is the means by which the Downer information reached the FBI. The United States is part of Five Eyes, an intelligence network that includes the United Kingdom, Canada, Australia, and New Zealand. The Five Eyes agreement is that any intelligence of note to partners is sent to, handled by, and transmitted by the country that gathered it. This helps guarantee that information is securely managed by trained professionals and subject to quality control; the system exists in part to guard against political manipulation. If Downer had concerns about Papadopoulos, his obligation was to report to Australian intelligence and let them handle it. But we know it wasn't Australian intelligence that alerted the FBI.

Instead, Downer decided to convey his information directly to the U.S. embassy in London. Meaning, to the Obama State Department. The Downer details landed with the embassy's then–chargé d'affaires, Elizabeth Dibble, who had previously served as a principal deputy assistant secretary in Clinton's State Department. This raises the alarming prospect that Obama political players were given this information early on, and added pressure to the FBI to act. It's hard to otherwise explain the Bureau's decision to go DEFCON 1 on the basis of such pathetically thin gruel.

* * *

What did the FBI actually have at the end of July 2016, on the eve of its official probe? It had suspicions about Page and Manafort, though (as made clear by the Mueller report) no real evidence. It had a dossier of wild accusations, though it was aware this had come from the Clinton camp. It had a tip from a foreign diplomat about the knowledge of a minor campaign aide, though the details amounted to little. All of this might have warranted—again—a defensive briefing for the Trump campaign, or even some follow-up. Instead, the FBI did something it had never done before, breaking perhaps one of the biggest rules of all: It launched a counterintelligence investigation into a domestic political campaign.

The public has never fully appreciated how dishonest this was. The FBI didn't have a crime to investigate. Page had broken no laws in going to Moscow; people do it all the time. Papadopoulos had broken no laws in talking to a work colleague who had Russian associates. The FBI didn't even have evidence to suggest a crime. Mueller ultimately contemplated more than a dozen statutes under which he might charge those Trump team members who interacted with Russians—from conspiracy laws to campaign finance rules—and couldn't find anything that stuck. The FBI knew it would have a hard time in a criminal investigation getting courts to sign off on anything, given its pathetic evidence and given the protections the U.S. Constitution affords U.S. citizens. So it instead launched a counterintelligence probe, which gave it greater latitude—additional tools and additional secrecy—to go after the Trump campaign.

When then–House Intelligence Chairman Nunes found out in January 2017 that the FBI was engaged specifically in a counterintelligence operation, he was stunned. He had for years sat on the committee charged with reviewing and updating the laws that give the intelligence community surveillance and metadata tools. "I would never have conceived of the FBI using our counterintelligence capabilities to target a political campaign," he told me. "If

it had crossed any of our minds, I can guarantee we'd have specifically written: 'Don't do that.'"

Having opened an inexcusable counterintelligence probe, the
FBI then went on to use inexcusable methods. According to press
reports, among these was the deployment of at least two human
informants—or rather, "spies"—against Trump campaign members. J. Edgar Hoover put the dirt he came across on politicians
in files, but even he, so far as we know, never sent spies into a political campaign.

Stefan Halper is an American foreign policy scholar at the
University of Cambridge and had likely been on the U.S. intelligence community's payroll for some time. At some point,
according to reports, Halper was tasked with reaching out to
Trump officials, under the ruse of discussing foreign policy. He
contacted Sam Clovis, the national co-chairman of the Trump
campaign, and the two met in late August or early September
in Virginia. In September, Halper sent an unsolicited e-mail to
Papadopoulos, asking him to London and offering to pay him
$3,000 to write a paper on foreign policy issues. Papadopoulos
later said that Halper grilled him on Clinton's hacked e-mails and
Russia's involvement, and that he responded that he knew nothing about that issue.

But the oddest Halper interaction involves Page, and it highlights the trouble with the FBI's origin story. The FBI officially
launched its probe on July 31, 2016, just a few days after it says
it received its information from Downer. And it still claims Papadopoulos was the reason for its probe. But we know that Halper
met Page in mid-July—weeks before the FBI launched its probe.
And the invitation Page received to the event where he met Halper
came even earlier—at the end of May or early June. Page had been
invited to a symposium at Cambridge, hosted by the Centre for
Research in the Arts, Sciences and Humanities (CRASSH). The
invitation came from the official organizer of the symposium, an
American academic named Steven Schrage, but the event was sup-

ported by Halper's department. Halper not only talked to Page at that event, but would continue talking to him into 2017.

Halper's very early outreach to Page is curious for another reason. Halper also has ties that lead back to Fusion. One of the participants in the July symposium Page attended was Sir Richard Dearlove, a Cambridge alumnus and the former chief of MI6. Dearlove and Halper know each other well, having run together the Cambridge Intelligence Seminar, an academic forum for researchers and one-time practitioners of spycraft. And, of course, Dearlove had been Steele's boss. Was Steele or Fusion using connections to conduct their own freelance spying or entrapment? That remains an open question.

* * *

What FBI rules was Halper operating under while he was interacting with Trump officials? Halper was supposed to be gathering information about a very specific topic: Russia. Did he talk about broader issues? If he was wearing a wire, did he turn it off during those discussions? If Halper reported back to the FBI any details of the Trump team's campaign strategy, the federal government would stand accused of snooping on the political activities of a candidate.

We already know the FBI failed to exert quality control over other sources, with dire consequences. Steele, as an official source, was subject to specific FBI regulations. Among these was the requirement that he keep confidential the information he shared with the FBI. Instead, he and Simpson in September 2016 began briefing significant numbers of the media about the dossier.

Those meetings helped publicly launch the Trump-Russia collusion narrative in the run-up to Election Day. On September 23, Michael Isikoff of *Yahoo! News* ran a story titled "U.S. Intel Officials Probe Ties Between Trump Adviser and Kremlin." The story explained that "U.S." officials had "received intelligence reports" about Page and Russians, and went on to recite verbatim several of the dossier's main allegations. Isikoff attributed the information to a "well-placed Western intelligence source," making it sound as if the dossier had come from someone in government, rather than an ex-spy and private gun-for-hire.

The story served as the Clinton campaign's early October surprise. Team Clinton jumped all over the report, highlighting the government investigation, never mind that the "intelligence" had been funded by its own camp. Jennifer Palmieri, the Clinton campaign communications director, took to TV to breathlessly highlight that "intelligence officials" were very worried about the Trump campaign. Other Clinton surrogates fanned out on social media to spread the allegations. The FBI, by accepting an opposition-research document from the Clinton campaign, provided that same campaign the opportunity to present Trump as in the FBI's crosshairs.

The Clinton camp got an additional political assist from a Democratic partisan, CIA Chief Brennan. Brennan by his own admission was deeply involved from the start in the Trump-Russia narrative. In May 2017 House testimony, Brennan bragged that he'd got the FBI wheels rolling. He explained that he'd "become aware of intelligence and information about contact between Russian officials and U.S. persons." The CIA is strictly barred from investigating U.S. citizens, but Brennan explained that he made sure that "every information and bit of intelligence" was "shared with the [FBI]." This information, he said, "served as the basis for the FBI investigation."

The admission highlights that Comey and the FBI weren't alone in their Trump harassment. Brennan early on began pushing the line that Russia was interfering in the election solely to aid Trump. His problem is that even his fellow intelligence heads wouldn't buy it. Asked about that theory in July 2016, Director of National Intelligence James Clapper publicly refused to say who was responsible for the hack of the DNC or what had motivated it. The FBI also took the position that Russian cyberattacks were aimed at disrupting the political system in general. Yet other analysts noted that Russian efforts to undermine Clinton—who Putin undoubtedly assumed would become president—were not the same thing as "help" for Trump.

Brennan nonetheless wanted his narrative out there, and so pulled an outrageous stunt. In late August, he "briefed" then–Senate minority leader Harry Reid, telling him that Putin was helping Trump, and that Trump advisers might be colluding with Russia. Within a few days, Reid had written a letter to Comey—which was immediately leaked to the press. "The evidence of a direct connection between the Russian government and Donald Trump's presidential campaign continues to mount," he wrote. He laid out the Russians-are-helping-Trump theory. He also publicly divulged at least one of the allegations in the dossier, those about Page's meetings in Moscow, and insisted the FBI use "every resource available to investigate this matter." With one meeting, Brennan had spread the word to more Democrats and the public about the dossier and increased pressure on the FBI to act.

* * *

Not that the FBI needed much prodding. It was already using informants. It was also using national security letters, which are a secret type of subpoena that allows the feds to obtain phone records and documents. Reports suggest the Bureau was collecting all these records against Manafort, Page, Papadopoulos, and Trump adviser and former general Michael Flynn. In October, it went even further, filing an application with the Foreign Intelligence Surveillance Court for permission to electronically surveil Page.

The federal government's power to eavesdrop on American citizens is among its scariest, which is why it is governed by strict rules. Think about how freaked out average Americans are by tech companies invading their privacy. Now imagine the listener is Big Brother. The FISA court was created in 1978 and exists to approve or deny government applications to surveil individuals who are suspected of being agents of a foreign power. FISA warrants allow for far more sweeping collection of material than do normal criminal wiretaps. Which is why it is supposed to be tough to obtain a FISA warrant, especially on an American citizen. Unfortunately, the FISA court generally approves everything tossed to it. Remember the old joke that a good prosecutor can get a grand jury to indict a ham sandwich? Even an inept Justice Department official can get a FISA judge to grant a deeply flawed surveillance application. Unlike normal courts, the FISA court doesn't have competing pleaders. The FBI and the Justice Department appear ex parte (without opponents) to make their case, and in secret, and the justices depend entirely on their candor.

Thanks to the public release of redacted versions of the Page applications, we now know what FBI "candor" looks like. More than half of the application's sixty-six pages were devoted to technical matters and a history of Russian electoral interference. Of the some twenty-five pages that focused on Page, much of it details his dealings with Russians. The key part of the application was its evidence section, titled "Page's Coordination with Russian Government Officials on 2016 U.S. Presidential Election Influence Activities." This bit was heavily redacted, but was almost entirely dossier-related.

The FBI's *Domestic Investigations and Operations Guide* clearly states that "only documented and verified information may be used to support FBI applications" to the FISA court. Yet former FBI investigator Bill Priestap acknowledged in testimony that at the time of the FISA application, the FBI's efforts to corroborate the dossier were in their "infancy," and we know that even Mueller could never substantiate the lies. Nonetheless, the FBI's application boldly declared in its opening pages to the court that "the target of this application" is "an agent of a foreign power" and went on to back that up with unverified accusations from the rival campaign.

The FBI meanwhile deliberately hid from the court the truth of who had paid for the dossier. It explained that it obtained information from "Source #1," who is clearly Steele. The report then contains a highly convoluted footnote that refers to "Source #1" and a "U.S.-based law firm" (Perkins Coie) as well as an "identified U.S. person" (Simpson) who was "likely" interested in discrediting "Candidate #1." Got that? All this is followed by another footnote in which the FBI hastens to say that despite the motivations of the "identified U.S. person," "Source #1" is "credible."

FBI supporters would later point out that FISA applications never contain names, and suggest all this coding and subterfuge was normal. Hardly. The application refers to "Candidate #1" (Trump) and "Political Party #1" (Republicans). The obvious and appropriate thing for the FBI to do was to make clear to the court that the information it was offering had been paid for by "Candidate #2" (Clinton) and "Political Party #2" (DNC). It did not. Baker, the FBI counsel, told Congress that the Page application was one of the few he ever personally reviewed, because it was so "sensitive" and "controversial." The FBI knew exactly what it was doing in keeping the details from the court.

But that wasn't the end of the FBI's deception. The Bureau was well aware of the *Yahoo! News* article in September that had quoted a "well-placed Western intelligence source," exposed its probe, and made public the dossier allegations. Anyone with a brain would know that the source was Steele, and that he had broken an FBI cardinal rule by running to the press. It isn't clear if the FBI failed to ask Steele about the story, or if Steele concealed his involvement from the FBI. Either way, there was plenty of reason for the Bureau to refrain from touting Steele's "credibility" in its FISA application. Not only did it go out of its way to present Steele in the best light, but the FBI included the *Yahoo! News* story in its application as additional evidence of Page's guilt—even though it came from the exact same source (Steele). DOJ Inspector General Michael Horowitz's December 2019 report into FISA abuse found that the FBI's initial Page application to the secret court contained no fewer than seven critical "errors or omissions," and ten more in the three subsequent applications.

* * *

FBI directors are given ten-year terms. The theory is that this long tenure helps to inoculate this powerful post from political pressure. Comey exposed the flip side: FBI directors are, in fact, inoculated from accountability.

Comey was ferociously disdainful of candidate Trump, one of the earliest manifestations of the Resistance. He was willing to believe the worst, and also willing to use his awesome powers to go after the Trump team. Puffed up on his own power, convinced he was saving the nation from a scourge, Comey flouted all the rules the FBI maintains to protect both its reputation and the citizenry.

And so, under the cloak of secrecy, the FBI head and his inner circle ran the first ever counterintelligence investigation into a nominee for the presidency. Along the way they ignored basic procedures governing political sensitivities, surveillance, sources, and methods. Comey allied his Bureau with a rival campaign, turning the FBI into a vessel for political skullduggery. These actions alone were enough to destroy public trust in a vital U.S. institution. But Comey was only getting started.

CHAPTER 4

SETTING UP A PRESIDENT

The FBI's anti-Trump campaign was primarily fueled by disdain and arrogance. But Comey and his team had one further thing pushing them to extremes: the belief that they'd never be caught.

Remember, the bulk of the FBI's rule-breaking—its failure with sources, its use of a counterintelligence investigation, its misuse of informants, its misinformation to the FISA court—happened at a time when every poll said Trump would lose the election decisively. Comey in TV appearances has acknowledged that the entire FBI top brass assumed Clinton would become president. "All of us were operating in a world where the polls were showing that Donald Trump had no chance," Comey told ABC News chief anchor George Stephanopoulos in April 2018.

Practically, that meant the FBI leadership was operating in full belief that its shenanigans would remain secret. Comey's decision to open a counterintelligence investigation—rather than a criminal one—allowed the Bureau to put the entire probe under a protective cone.

Comey had meanwhile separately broken another rule by hiding his investigation from Congress. The FBI routinely briefs senior and intelligence committee members of the House and Senate about sensitive counterintelligence investigations. These briefings aren't a matter of courtesy; they are necessary both for information-sharing and oversight. They inform the elected branch of security risks and threats from hostile actors as it goes about legislation. And they allow Congress to pass along to intelligence agencies the information it obtains via foreign contacts and tips. The briefings are also the means by which Congress ensures that the intelligence community isn't abusing its authority under counterintelligence statutes. The more sensitive the investigation, the greater the obligation of the FBI to let Congress know. Comey instead testified that he deliberately kept his investigation secret from Congress on the grounds that it was simply *too* sensitive—an absurd argument.

Meanwhile, the FBI's decision to withhold from the FISA court the dirty details of the Clinton dossier meant that the other potential check on FBI power—the judicial branch—was also in the dark about key details. All this guaranteed that no one other than the incoming Clinton administration would ever know how the FBI had spied on the Trump team.

Trump's victory destroyed this scenario, bringing with it an alarming new FBI reality: Within a few months a Republican president would know all the gory details. That reality brought with it a panic and a high-stakes FBI and Obama administration strategy—to take down or disable a new president. Those actions further destroyed trust in the FBI, the Justice Department, and the intelligence community, even as they severely undermined the powers of the presidency in ways that could dog generations of chief executives to come.

* * *

The FBI leadership's first reaction to the Trump win was to double down on its investigation. The FBI's Russia investigation team ramped up for a second surveillance warrant against Page. It also broke more rules about sourcing. The FBI had finally fired Steele, after his press blabbing grew too brazen to ignore. Steele had given an interview on October 31, 2016, to *Mother Jones* writer David Corn. Dismissed for having violated FBI source rules about the press, the FBI had no business dealing with Steele—and the Bureau knew it.

Which is why the Trump-probe team instead turned to a cutout—Bruce Ohr. And Ohr remained in contact with Steele. Steele continued to dump his dirt with Ohr, and Ohr continued to funnel it to the FBI. From November 2016 through spring 2017, the FBI officially pumped Ohr for his Steele-Fusion info in at least a dozen interviews. Ohr also remained in contact with Glenn Simpson. At least Steele had once been an FBI source; Simpson was a political operator.

The FBI also briefed members of the Obama administration about its work, enabling them to begin their own outrageous surveillance of incoming Trump administration players. The Department of Justice and the FBI have always been cagey about just how much the Obama White House knew about the Trump investigation prior to the election. Comey certainly briefed NSA principals in the spring about the FBI's suspicions, and he has dropped other hints that the Obama team was getting updates.

But there is no question the Obama White House was given all the ugly details after the election—as this is when they started snooping on the very same people the FBI was targeting. Our intelligence community routinely listens to the telephone conversations of foreign nationals, especially those with potential hostile intentions. The intelligence community writes up summaries. If the intelligence community is listening to a conversation between a foreign national and a U.S. citizen, it by law is required to "minimize" the identity of the American. This requirement exists to prevent the government from using these tools as a backdoor method of invading the privacy of U.S. citizens. Senior members of administrations nonetheless have the power to "unmask"—or demand to see the identity of—the Americans listed in the reports. This can be done only by high-ranking officials, who are supposed to provide a serious legal argument for the privacy intrusion. It is also meant to be exceptionally rare.

In the months following Trump's victory, members of the Obama White House made hundreds of unmasking demands, allowing them to read word-for-word the conversations the incoming presidential team was having with outsiders. Most of these unmaskings requests were boilerplate and did not list specific reasons for why the officials needed the information. The team received dozens of other summaries that technically "masked" Trump team members but also made obvious who they were. Many of the reports contained political information about the transition team's meetings and policy plans—nothing to do with Russia. All this was a clear abuse of the unmasking rules.

At least one of the unmaskings came at the hands of former Obama National Security Advisor Susan Rice. This was odd, as Ms. Rice's job was policy advice—she was not engaged in counter-intelligence investigations. She later insisted she has not done the unmasking for "any political purposes." Both former Deputy Attorney General Sally Yates and DNI Clapper also admitted to personally reviewing classified documents in which Trump, his associates, or members of Congress had been unmasked, and both admitted to sharing the details with other members of the Obama government. Yet the bulk of the unmaskings came via an official with absolutely zero cause to make them: former United Nations ambassador Samantha Power. Power was a diplomat with no intelligence-related function in government; nothing about her job required unmasking, as she herself seemed to later acknowledge. Power on paper made as many as 260 unmasking requests, but she later told Congress that she wasn't technically responsible for many of them; someone had done them in her name. Documents released in May 2020 show thirty-nine Obama officials unmasked Mr. Flynn alone.

We also don't know how much of this was part of a corrupt practice known as "reverse surveillance." It's (supposed to be) hard to get the FISA court to give permission to surveil a U.S.

citizen. But political actors long ago figured a workaround. They first take educated guesses about who their target U.S. citizen might be talking to outside the country. They then create a pretext to listen in on that foreigner. Voilà, they have the conversations of the U.S. citizen. The sheer number of Obama unmaskings suggests that at least some of these tapped conversations were reverse engineered. In short, both the FBI and the Obama team were desperately monitoring the Trump transition for anything that might belatedly derail a Trump presidency.

* * *

At the same time, the FBI and the Obama White House rushed to get out ahead of the storyline. They needed to further flame the "Trump-Russia" collusion theory and release damning accusations, the better to justify their election-year actions. This campaign culminated in a one-two punch on the day of January 6, 2017.

Brennan had pushed the intelligence community to embrace his Putin-aiding-Trump-specifically theme, but hadn't got traction during the election season. Now the administration went all in. By December, according to the *Washington Post*, Obama had ordered "a comprehensive review by U.S. intelligence agencies into Russian interference in U.S. elections." The principals scrambled to use this as the vehicle to launch Brennan's views publicly, as an official intelligence product, released on January 6. The *Post* story noted that this new report "was based largely on the work done by the task force Brennan had established and made public what the CIA had concluded in August, that 'Putin and the Russian government aspired to help President-elect Trump's election chances when possible by discrediting Secretary Clinton.'"

But it was the administration's other big move on January 6 that truly launched the Trump-Russia narrative into the stratosphere. The day before, January 5, Comey and Acting Attorney

General Sally Yates met with Obama, Biden, and Rice. The discussion was about how much to tell the president-elect about its Russia investigation. The correct answer, of course, should have been "everything." The FBI has to this day insisted its investigation was only into specific individuals in the campaign—not into the campaign itself or Trump. As the incoming president, Trump had a vital stake in, and right to know, any of the FBI's concerns about his team—in particular any issues with incoming National Security Advisor Michael Flynn.

The audacious decision was made to instead mislead Trump—the man the public had just elected president, the man who would in mere weeks be Comey's boss. On that January 6, Comey, Brennan, Clapper, and National Security Agency head Mike Rogers provided President-Elect Trump a "briefing." The intelligence chiefs told Trump only about their concerns about Russian interference—not that the FBI was specifically looking into whether the campaign had "colluded." Comey then also gave Trump a deliberately deceptive description of the dossier. He told the president-elect *only* about the dossier's allegations that Trump cavorted with prostitutes in a Moscow hotel, on the supposed grounds that Trump needed to "know" such a salacious allegation existed. He did not tell the president-elect about the dossier's claims that the Trump campaign was colluding with Russia, nor did he tell the president that this packet of opposition research was a central plank of an FBI investigation into the Trump campaign. Comey's decision to provide such an incomplete briefing to an incoming president—to deliberately withhold crucial information from Trump and his team—was scandalous. FBI directors are not chosen by the public; they remain subordinate to elected officials. Comey's move to hide his Bureau's work from the incoming commander in chief is an abuse of power potentially unrivaled in recent political times.

All the more so given that the briefing seemed primarily a means for Comey to get the dossier out to the public. Comey was well aware the media was in possession of the dossier. But even the low-standard Beltway press corps had been reluctant to publish its crazed allegations. It needed an excuse. As liberal commentator Matt Taibbi noted in his book *Hate Inc.*, Mr. Comey's dossier briefing was the classic Washington "trick." It served as the "pretext" to get the details out, a "news hook" to allow the press to publish the dossier. Indeed, within hours of Comey's "private" briefing, the press was buzzing with reports that the FBI director had informed the president of sensitive allegations made against him. And not long after, BuzzFeed had decided the public deserved to know what those allegations were.

Between its intelligence assessment and the publication of the dossier, the Obama team had effectively set the narrative: Putin had wanted Trump to win, and the Trump campaign may have accepted Putin's help. The Russia-collusion narrative was off to the races. But Comey had taken one last incredibly important action—deliberate, and again, unconscionable—that helped guarantee it would continue. Congressional Republicans had also demanded Comey provide them a briefing on the dossier. According to Devin Nunes, Comey at that briefing repeated his claim that Republicans had paid for the dossier. "If they had informed us Hillary Clinton and the Democrats paid for that dossier, I can guarantee you that Mitch McConnell and Paul Ryan would have laughed and walked out of that meeting," Nunes told me. He's right. They'd have walked, they'd have blown the whistle, and the entire Trump-Russia charade would have ended before it began. Instead, Comey and his FBI kept quiet about the dossier's origins—and laid their next traps.

* * *

The first to get snared was retired U.S. Army Lt. General Michael Flynn. Flynn had served his country honorably for more than thirty years as a paratrooper and in military intelligence. Obama

in April 2012 nominated him as the head of the Defense Intelligence Agency, where his sweeping plans to change the way
that body worked instantly earned him enemies throughout the
Obama administration and defense structure. Flynn was ultimately forced out of the DIA in 2014, notably in part because
of the meddling of one Stefan Halper—the same FBI-CIA asset
who helped inform on the Trump campaign. Halper had organized one of their intelligence seminars in Cambridge in 2014,
and Flynn was invited to speak. A colleague of Halper's reported
back to the U.S. government that Halper had thought Flynn was
too cozy with a Russian woman who was also in attendance.

Flynn, a registered Democrat, remained a respected military
figure in Republican circles and was consulted by GOP presidential candidates ranging from Scott Walker to Ted Cruz. He
ultimately joined the Trump campaign as an adviser in February
2016. Obama partisans were furious when he gave a cutting
speech at the August Republican convention, accusing his former
bosses of craven foreign policy. He also slammed Clinton, noting
that if he (a former intelligence official) had done "a tenth" of
what she'd done mishandling classified information, he'd "be in
jail." Flynn clearly incensed Team Obama, to the extent that
Obama personally trashed Flynn to President-Elect Trump when
the two met a few days after the election. Obama, according to
Politico, warned Trump not to hire Flynn, accusing him of being "problematic" and having "crazy ideas." Yet Obama certainly
never suggested Flynn was a Russian asset, and the Obama administration had never taken any steps to revoke Flynn's high-level
security clearance.

We don't know how early Flynn became a Comey suspect, but
senior government leaders started listening in on his conversations not long after Trump's November 2016 appointment of him
as national security advisor. It's also unclear if the FBI directly
tapped him with a FISA warrant, or if he was being picked up as
part of intelligence monitoring of foreign nationals that he was

speaking to—or both. But the administration became aware of a December 29, 2016, conversation Flynn had with the Russian ambassador to the United States, Sergey Kislyak. It happened on the same day that the Obama administration imposed sanctions on Russia for its interference in the 2016 election. The incoming Trump administration was concerned the sanctions would harm their incoming relationship with Russia, and Flynn in the call requested that the Russians not escalate. By January 2, the Obama White House knew of this conversation, and by January 12, "a senior U.S. government official" had leaked the fact of the Flynn call to *Washington Post* columnist David Ignatius. Ignatius also used his column to lay the groundwork for the ludicrous claim that Flynn had broken . . . the Logan Act of 1799.

The Logan Act is an ancient law that criminalizes negotiation by unauthorized persons with foreign governments that are in dispute with the United States. Only two defendants have ever been charged under the Logan Act—the more recent one in 1852—and neither was convicted. It is absolutely normal for members of a presidential transition team to talk to their foreign counterparts, and on all manner of subjects.

Yet the Obama administration seized on the Logan Act as a pretext to escalate its investigation of the Trump team and to further fan the Russia-collusion flames. Indeed, it was on Logan Act grounds that Comey's FBI set about entrapping Flynn. On January 24, mere days after he was sworn in, Flynn got a call from Deputy FBI Director Andy McCabe, ostensibly to talk about an FBI training session. But then McCabe slipped in that he felt the FBI needed to have a few agents talk to Flynn about his Russia communications.

It says something appalling about Comey's FBI and its tactics that the only purpose of this meeting was to put Flynn in legal jeopardy. The FBI did not need to ask Flynn about the nature of his Russian communications. It already had all the transcripts. It knew exactly what he had said. Moreover, McCabe urged Flynn to meet without a lawyer. "I explained that I thought the quickest way to get this done was to have a conversation between [Flynn] and the agents only. I further stated that if LTG Flynn wished to include anyone else in the meeting, like the White House Counsel for instance, that I would need to involve the Department of Justice. [Flynn] stated that this would not be necessary and agreed to meet with the agents without any additional participants." This setup was Comey's idea. Comey would brag to MSNBC in 2018 that it was "something I probably wouldn't have done or wouldn't have gotten away with in a more organized administration." He said: "In the George W. Bush Administration or the Obama Administration, if the FBI wanted to send agents into the White House itself to interview a senior official, you would work through the White House counsel, there would be discussions and approval about who would be there. And I thought, it's early enough, let's just send a couple guys over."

McCabe meanwhile recounted that he and FBI officials also decided that they would deliberately "not warn Flynn that it was a crime to lie during an FBI interview because they wanted Flynn to be relaxed." And rather than flag the transcript for Flynn and ask him for an explanation, the agents (one of whom was Peter Strzok) decided before the meeting that if Flynn did not confirm what he had said in the conversation, "they would not confront him or talk him through it."

Flynn for his part had no reason to be alarmed; the FBI's Russia probe was still secret, and Flynn had done absolutely nothing wrong in speaking to the Russian ambassador. Indeed the agents reported back that he'd been helpful. They'd shown up within hours of McCabe's call and found Flynn had been "relaxed and jocular" and "clearly saw the FBI agents as allies." When asked whether he'd asked the Russians not to escalate the situation, Flynn responded: "Not really. I don't remember. It wasn't 'Don't do anything.'"

This is hardly a definitive "no." And there's good reason to believe Flynn didn't remember. As a former intelligence official, Flynn would have known the U.S. government was listening to Kislyak and likely heard his conversation—he'd have no reason to lie. In the months leading up to the inauguration, he'd also had hundreds of calls with foreign leaders on hundreds of subjects. In the wake of the Ignatius column, Flynn had similarly told Trump officials he hadn't discussed sanctions. Most important, the FBI agents themselves did not think Flynn was lying. The FBI summary reported that "both had the impression at the time that Flynn was not lying or did not think he was lying."

But none of this was good enough for then–acting AG Sally Yates, who soon after the FBI interview demanded an emergency meeting with White House Counsel Don McGahn. Yates laid out her wild Logan Act theory. She also claimed that Flynn had lied to the vice president and the FBI, and that the Russians knew it, which meant Flynn had been "compromised" and was vulnerable to blackmail.

Several weeks on, Obama partisans remained frustrated that they hadn't taken out their man—so they went to the press. In a coordinated attack, both the *Washington Post* and the *New York Times* on February 9 reported exact pieces of Flynn's conversation with Kislyak in December. The *Washington Post* spewed the Logan Act line, claiming the conversation was "inappropriate and potentially illegal." Nunes, the head of the House Intelligence Committee, would later call the leak the most destructive to national security he'd seen in his time in Washington—given its exposure of technical methods. The leaking of classified information—which the Kislyak-Flynn conversation most certainly counts as—is a felony punishable with up to ten years in federal prison. The *Post*'s version of the story bragged that it had been sourced by no less than *nine* separate officials. And it worked. Within a week, the White House had fired Flynn for lying to the vice president.

* * *

The Flynn leak story is important because it highlights yet another way the Resistance wreaked lasting damage on the country—in particular on institutions of national security and our relationships with crucial foreign allies. As former NSA head Mike Rogers once explained, leaks "reveal the sources and methods we employ to provide intelligence to American policymakers and warfighters and generate advantage for our nation while protecting its citizens." Intelligence professionals get particularly alarmed by the mishandling of information about U.S. citizens, because it rightly undermines trust in the government and puts at risk the surveillance tools the professionals need to keep track of legitimate bad guys. Foreign partners also grow reluctant to share information with any country that can't be counted on to keep secrets. All this is why no less than Jim Comey once testified that "leaks of classified information are serious, serious federal crimes for a reason."

Yet the Trump haters were so intent on bringing down the early Trump administration that they put into place an official new structure that guaranteed the ensuing volley of leaks. As the *New York Times* reported in March 2017, Obama "White House officials scrambled" in their last days to "spread information" about "possible contacts between associates of President-elect Donald J. Trump and Russians—across the government," so as to "leave a clear trail of intelligence for government investigators." At intelligence agencies, the story reported, "there was a push to process as much raw intelligence as possible into analyses, and to keep the reports at a relatively low classification level to ensure as wide a readership as possible across the government—and, in some cases, among European allies."

Only days before Trump's inauguration, Obama also signed an executive order that allowed the National Security Agency to share raw intercepts and data with the sixteen other agencies in the intelligence community. The new order vastly increased the number of intelligence analysts who had access to this raw NSA surveillance. NSA analysts once filtered out irrelevant information and minimized the names of American citizens. Under the Obama rules, it was out there for the taking.

The leaks that accompanied the first part of the Trump administration were so numerous and damaging that Senate Homeland Security and Governmental Affairs Chairman Ron Johnson felt compelled to study it. His team examined media leaks between January 20, 2017, and May 25, 2017—Trump's first 126 days in office. The report found the Trump administration had "faced 125 leaked stories—one leak a day—containing information that is potentially damaging to national security under the standards laid out in a 2009 Executive Order signed by President Barack Obama." The leaking was seven times faster than that in Obama's first 126 days. Nearly 80 percent of the leaks focused on the Russia probe, and many revealed "closely-held information such as intelligence community intercepts, FBI interviews and intelligence, grand jury subpoenas, and even the workings of a secret surveillance court."

One leak revealed that Trump may have shared classified information with the Russians. A subsequent leak revealed that Israel had provided the intelligence Trump shared. The latter leak caused a diplomatic incident and led to Israel's decision to change the way it shared information with the United States. As *Washington Post* columnist Marc Thiessen wrote: "Ponder the irony: These geniuses were so appalled by Trump sharing sensitive intelligence with the Russians that they shared even more sensitive intelligence with the media—and thus the entire world—in order to demonstrate that Trump cannot be trusted with sensitive intelligence. In doing so, these leakers possibly did far more damage to U.S. national security—and intelligence-sharing between the United States and Israel—than anything Trump may have revealed to the Russians."

Equally damaging was Comey's refusal to do anything about the illegal disclosures. The FBI director's reaction to the Flynn leak is a reminder that officials can abuse their position by ignoring laws just as much as they can by flouting them. Leaks are in the FBI's purview, and that initial, jaw-dropping Flynn leak would have been easy to track down. The government keeps records of unmasking requests; Comey's FBI could have tracked down who unmasked Flynn and then followed the information from there.

Yet at a House hearing in March 2016, Comey refused to even acknowledge he was looking into the leaks. Sources later told me that Comey also willfully obstructed Congress's own investigation into the leaks. He refused requests for documents that would have shown who had unmasked Flynn. And he refused to provide the name in a closed-door meeting with senior congressional leaders. This led some Republicans to note that the FBI is one of the agencies with the power to unmask. Indeed, it later came out that Comey was among the officials who unmasked Flynn.

Either way, Mr. Comey never showed interest in sleuthing down the Flynn leakers. Had the FBI taken quick action and set an example of the offenders, it would have deterred the flood of criminal leaks that continues against the Trump administration even today. Those include everything from leaked transcripts of Trump's calls with foreign leaders, to the leaked names of FBI sources. In April 2019, the Federation of American Scientists, which keeps track of the intelligence community, reported that the Justice Department had received over the prior two years a record number of referrals for leak prosecutions. The DOJ received 120 leak referrals in 2017 and 88 in 2018. By comparison, it received 37 in 2016 (Obama's last year) and 18 in 2015. As of this writing, no one has been held accountable for the Flynn leak.

* * *

The dossier release and the takedown of Flynn helped the haters cement in the public conscience the notion of a Trump-Russia collusion. The next takedown, of Attorney General Jeff Sessions, served an additional purpose—it guaranteed that nobody outside the Department of Justice would exert independent oversight over an out-of-control operation.

This was the goal all along. Sessions had barely been sworn in before Democrats were demanding his recusal, on the grounds that he'd been too close to the Trump campaign to fairly investigate the Trump-Russia collusion story. Sessions had (rightly) resisted those calls. His opponents finally found their leverage. On March 1, 2017, in the wake of the Flynn resignation, the *Washington Post* reported that Sessions "spoke twice last year" with Kislyak, and moreover that he "did not disclose" this supposedly vital information during his confirmation hearings. It turns out Sessions was asked during the hearing if in his capacity as a Trump surrogate he'd had contact with the Russian government. He'd said no, and this was absolutely true. He'd met with Kislyak briefly on two occasions in his capacity as a sitting U.S. senator—once at a 2016 summer reception, and once in the not-so-secret confines of his Senate office. Democrats didn't care about the distinction, and within a day of the uproar over the *Post* story, Sessions had formally recused himself from overseeing the Trump-Russia investigation. Democrats were so vicious that they'd go on to demand that Comey's FBI open a criminal perjury investigation into Sessions.

This hobbling of Sessions is even more outrageous in hindsight. Don't forget: A lot of Democrats in Washington at this point likely knew that their party had a hand in the dossier. Certainly members of the Obama administration and Clinton campaign did. How far had the information traveled? How many elected officials in early 2016 calling for a Sessions recusal were doing so in an effort to ensure no Trump official got wind of their actions? Also don't forget that at this time, not a single Republican knew the truth of the dossier. Republicans had read the Buzz-Feed release, but according to Comey, it had been funded by conservatives. Republicans knew that Democrats' demands for Sessions's recusal were silly; they didn't know the demands were self-serving.

His removal left Comey free to operate at will. And while Comey's investigatory steps continued apace, he also continued his dishonest interactions with his new boss—Donald Trump. Comey's actions, as would later become clear, were highly political and all aimed at undermining a new president.

In his January 6 briefing of Trump about the dossier, Comey had offered a personal assurance that Trump was not the subject of any investigation. He repeated that assurance during a dinner with Trump on January 27. Trump continued to be appalled over the dossier allegations about what went on in a Moscow hotel room and told Comey he was debating having the FBI investigate to prove they were untrue. Comey, according to his own notes, counseled that "he should give that careful thought because it might create a narrative that we were investigating him personally, which we weren't, and because it was very difficult to prove a negative."

Comey then appeared in front of the House Intelligence Committee on March 20, 2017, and took the extraordinary step of blaring out the news that the FBI was investigating "links between individuals associated with the Trump campaign and the Russian government." This was remarkable, given the government usually declines to confirm the existence of any investigation, much less a counterintelligence probe. The entire performance was a Comey political classic. He liberally handed out soundbites that Democrats could use to pump the collusion theory, even as he refused to offer any concrete details about what had happened or what the FBI knew. He specifically declined to answer whether the FBI had any evidence of collusion. By the end of the show, the thundercloud hanging over the Trump administration had darkened, and the president was understandably concerned.

Comey then reassured Trump for a third time: The FBI had

briefed congressional leadership on precisely who was being targeted, and Trump wasn't on that list.

Trump wanted Comey to state that publicly—but Comey
stubbornly refused. His excuse later was that he worried that if
he publicly struck Trump off his target list and later found information implicating him, it would create "a duty to correct."
Undoubtedly. But at the same time, the FBI director was holding
in his hands a crippling power over the office of the presidency.
He'd made public that the FBI was investigating officials connected to Trump. By this point, not one of the four individuals
originally targeted—Page, Manafort, Papadopoulos, Flynn—was
working with the administration. Yet Comey hung out the possi-
bility that even the president may be implicated. The uncertainty
surrounding this open-ended probe was already strangling the administration's ability to govern, and Comey had an unequivocal
duty to clear the air.

Even Comey admits that Trump welcomed an FBI probe into any
Trump associates who might have engaged in wrongdoing. But
Trump specifically asked Comey on several occasions to make public
the fact that the president wasn't under investigation—to remove
what Trump called the "cloud." Comey ignored him. He seemed to
want the president to labor under the burden of suspicion.

All along, we now know, Comey was memorializing every discussion he had with Trump. The memos are painful proof of just
how politically unaware Trump was in his first months in office.
He continued to speak frankly to everyone, even the politically
ruthless FBI director. Among the "scandalous" revelations in the
later Comey memos was that Trump had at one point told Comey
that Flynn was a "good guy" and that he hoped Comey could let
the issue "go." Trump had said the same flattering things publicly
about Flynn. But he should never have brought up that subject, or
Russia, or anything to do with ongoing investigations with Comey
the note-taking knife fighter. The G-man—who'd spent his life
putting people behind bars—was writing down every word.

Those memos are among the proof that Comey never treated Trump with the same deference that he afforded prior bosses, and that Comey's primary interest was Comey. If the director was as alarmed by Trump's comments about Flynn as he claimed to be in his memos, he had an obvious course. He had a legal duty to report it to his superiors and a moral duty to resign. Instead, he ferreted the information into a secret file. The memos were his insurance policy, potentially even leverage. He was laying down evidence he could use to protect his job, or to retaliate against Trump if he were fired. It had in it ugly echoes of J. Edgar Hoover, who used information his FBI collected against political rivals to inoculate himself from accountability.

Comey did get fired, of course. The *WSJ* editorial page had called for Trump to axe the FBI head the minute he'd taken office. He was already infamous for his ego, and his handling of the Clinton affair was proof that this self-regard had skewed the FBI's neutrality. The new administration didn't listen, and it was four long months before Deputy AG Rod Rosenstein—now in charge of Russian issues, given Sessions's recusal—issued his blistering memo explaining why Comey had to go. Rosenstein in his May 9 document laid out breaches of DOJ protocol in Comey's investigation of Clinton: The FBI's job is to make recommendations to DOJ prosecutors; Comey made the call on Clinton himself. The DOJ isn't in the business of airing dirty laundry; Comey held a July 2016 press conference in which he exonerated Clinton but also berated her behavior. The Rosenstein memo was more than compelling, and it cited former attorneys general and deputy attorneys general—from both sides of the aisle—who supported this judgment of Comey's behavior.

The firing on May 9, 2017, nonetheless set off the second major scandal narrative of the Trump administration: obstruction of justice. Democrats only a few months earlier were calling for Comey's head. Now the haters re-embraced the FBI director as a liberal martyr, claiming Trump had fired him to shut down the

Russia investigation, and that the Rosenstein memo was a cover-up. This argument was, of course, nuts; if Trump's goal was to obstruct the investigation, firing Comey was the dumbest way to do it. His termination guaranteed a seething new national obsession with the Trump-Russia collusion narrative.

Indeed, it pushed the FBI to even greater abuses of power. The FBI had up to then investigated the Trump campaign at large; soon after Comey's termination, his deputy, McCabe, ordered an investigation into the president himself. McCabe admitted the FBI had no evidence that Trump was knowingly working for Russians, but instead said they moved forward in part because of what they felt were concerning Trump comments—in public and private—about Russia. This was a dangerous rationale for an investigation—one that threatens future presidencies and foreign policy. Under the Constitution, the president alone has the authority to negotiate with foreign leaders. Presidents often engage in controversial interactions with their foreign counterparts, including rogue regimes. Nixon did so with China; more recently Obama did so with Iran. McCabe's decision suggested the FBI had the authority to judge those contacts and potentially declare them criminal. If the FBI can open an investigation directly into a president over his foreign policy actions, every future president must fear the consequences of making a controversial foreign policy decision. That is incredibly chilling, and a destabilizing encroachment on core presidential powers.

The probe also laid the groundwork for an official investigation into Trump over obstruction. McCabe would later claim he did all this because he was concerned Trump would try to shut the whole probe down. But this makes little sense, given that McCabe at the exact same moment (May 11) publicly testified to Congress that "there has been no effort to impede our investigation to date." The more likely and concerning scenario is that this was the FBI acting in retribution; Trump had fired its beloved leader, and now it was gunning for Trump.

And according to McCabe, that even included a stunning discussion in the days following Comey's firing as to how the FBI might engineer Trump's removal via the 25th Amendment. McCabe later said that Rosenstein raised this scenario, in the context of "thinking about how many other cabinet officials might support such an effort." (Rosenstein would claim that he was never in a "position to consider invoking the 25th Amendment" and also point out that McCabe was fired from the FBI for lying—though he didn't outright deny the discussion.) Assuming even a kernel of truth exists as to this conversation, it was as extraordinary as it was unprecedented. Trump was entirely within his constitutional prerogative to fire Comey, and yet Comey's associates immediately talked about deposing him in what would have amounted to a coup. The 25th Amendment was passed after JFK's assassination to allow for a transfer of power when a president is "unable" to discharge his duties. It's supposed to be used only after demonstrated evidence of impairment, witnessed by those closest to a president. It doesn't exist to settle political differences, or to allow scheming bureaucrats to nullify an election and decide who sits as president. The very conversation was an affront to the Constitution and another example of how an elitist political and media class has continued to pose a greater threat to norms than anything Trump is known to have done.

The greatest consequence of the Comey firing was that it allowed the now-disgraced FBI director, and fellow haters, to engineer a special counsel. One week after his firing, the *New York Times* reported on the Comey memos, including Trump's comments about Flynn. It later came out that Comey had orchestrated the leak. He'd provided the memos to a friend at Columbia Law School, using that cutout to get his information to the media. He'd also deliberately written some of the memos without classified information so that they could ultimately be made public—suggesting he'd been planning to use them all along. In one of his memos, Comey proudly recounts that he told Trump in early

2017: "I don't do sneaky things, I don't leak, I don't do weasel moves." Except, apparently, when he did.

Comey with his leak sent a message to the FBI ranks: It's okay to record conversations with politicians and make them public. Indeed, an Inspector General report criticized Comey for violating policies and for setting a "dangerous example" for the over 35,000 current FBI employees. This was Comey once again demonstrating that he didn't believe the normal rules applied to him. None in the Obama and Comey teams did, and they abused their positions to unmask, to place political opponents in legal peril, to leak, to subvert elected officials, and to undermine core powers of the executive branch. And the Resistance thinks Trump has overstepped boundaries?

Comey later explained his entire goal with the leak was "to prompt the appointment of a special counsel"—and it worked. Democrats had for months been demanding a special counsel or a select House-Senate investigation to look into the Trump-Russia claims, but Republicans had resisted. It was the memos—which had been deliberately written and leaked to present Trump as having engaged in obstruction from his first days in office—that tipped the scales. Rosenstein cracked: On May 17, 2017, the day after the leak, the deputy AG announced that former FBI Director Bob Mueller would investigate Trump-Russia ties. More than a year earlier, Comey had set his sights on Trump. He might be gone, but he'd successfully passed the torch to Mueller. The collusion-obstruction circus was on.

CHAPTER 5

MASTERS OF OBSTRUCTION

When next you are tempted to think of our federal legislative branch as dysfunctional and lazy—as we are all routinely tempted to do—spare a thought for the Russia investigators. This was one case of the public getting its taxpayer money's worth.

The American public only knows about the FBI's rogue operations because of a few resolute members of Congress. The House and Senate Republicans who exposed the 2016 abuses reminded the country of the indispensability of effective oversight. Their triumph is all the more notable given the haters' determination to deny them information. Justice Department and FBI partisans engaged in extraordinary acts of obstruction and undermined our constitutional separation of powers in ways that will haunt future Congresses and administrations.

Congressional Democrats in their own fervor to block discovery meanwhile destroyed the reputation of the few remaining "grown-up" committees in Congress. They flouted committee rules, setting dangerous new precedents for the future. And they weaponized the ethics process, using it to sideline Republican sleuths. The Democrats' desperation to cover up the real truth of the FBI's behavior—and to keep the Trump-Russia-collusion narrative rolling—marked the beginning of a new partisan low in

Congress, one that would grow worse with the return of Speaker Nancy Pelosi in 2019.

* * *

Devin Nunes knew that something was very weird, and very wrong, not long after the 2016 presidential election. He'd read the stories suggesting the FBI was looking into the Trump campaign but had dismissed them. He assumed that if the FBI was conducting a serious probe, it would have notified Congress. And as the head of the House Intelligence Committee, Nunes would have been the first to hear.

In the aftermath of the November vote, Nunes started noticing a sharp escalation of attacks against him on social media and outlets like MSNBC. Attacks were nothing new for the California congressman; it was the subject matter that was bizarre. Liberal commentators started claiming he was in cahoots with Russia. Nunes had been a Russia hawk in Congress long before Russia hawks were fashionable. Only six months earlier he'd issued a scathing appraisal of the Obama administration's Russia policy, calling the then-president's failure to understand Putin's plans and intentions one of the largest intelligence failures since 9/11. The attacks were so absurd, they made Nunes wonder what the hell was happening.

It would make sense only in retrospect, and that timing is an important part of the Trump-Russia collusion narrative. Remember, it would take Republicans nearly another year to discover that Clinton and the DNC were behind the dossier. In the first few months after the 2016 election, they weren't even aware the FBI was probing the Trump campaign. But Democrats knew. People in the Obama administration knew. People in the Clinton orbit knew. And certainly, as a result, Democratic members of Congress knew. Those congressional Democrats had engineered Sessions's recusal, to help protect the FBI's secrets. Now they needed to sideline any elected Republicans who might be in a position to find information.

At the top of their lists were the GOP heads of both the Senate and the House Intelligence Committees. And North Carolina Senator Richard Burr proved an easy mark. As soon as the haters had in early January established the Trump-Russia collusion narrative, they trained their fire on Burr, depicting him as a lackey of the incoming president. A *New York Times* story in February 2017 quoted Senate Democrats who argued any Burr inquiry would only be about a desire to "protect President Trump." Missouri's Claire McCaskill demanded a special committee to "investigate this matter in a thorough, public and responsible way." The Resistance claimed Burr was incapable of conducting a fair probe and had potentially even been co-opted by the White House to run interference.

Republicans were always correct in demanding they retain control over these investigations; it was the only appropriate venue to really dig into the scandal. Even early on, it was clear that both the Justice Department and the FBI were too conflicted to do a probe of their own actions. The FBI had engaged in some unusual behavior and was possibly the source of some of the criminal leaks. And the Sessions recusal meant no one from the outside would be taking a fresh look at the department. As Iowa Senator Chuck Grassley would later ask, with regard to the leaks: "So how can the Justice Department guarantee the integrity of the investigations without designating an agency, other than the FBI, to gather the facts and eliminate senior FBI officials as suspects?" Congress was the best thing going for accountability. Burr ultimately kept his investigation, though at the price of a promise to do the bidding of his committee Democrats—a mistake that would enable the left to further capitalize on its Trump-Russia narrative.

The real target was Nunes, who Democrats understood from the start would not be easily cowed. The Californian had been particularly troubled by the January and February leaks about Flynn; he suspected an inappropriate unmasking. But then he got tips from sources saying that Flynn was only the start; the Obama administration had been unmasking like mad. The sources provided him with information about specific documents that would prove it. Viewing those documents, however, required Nunes to go to a secure reading room on the White House grounds where the documents were stored. Nunes was as transparent as possible about this trip. On March 22, immediately after his examination, he called a press conference to publicly explain what he'd found: The Obama administration had unmasked Trump officials, and the information it collected had been widely dispersed across government, despite having "little or no intelligence value." Much of it, said Nunes, wasn't even related to Russia. Nunes then briefed the White House on his discovery.

But the haters jumped to claim that Nunes's trip had been orchestrated by Trump's inner circle, and that he was too partisan to lead a House probe. Democrats slammed him for not telling them about his findings first. They accused him of carrying water for the president, of undermining the committee's investigation, and of hiding details. The press gave full airing to these false claims, ignoring the fact that the Nunes discovery was unrelated to the "collusion" question that his committee was investigating. Nunes had obtained dozens of documents showing the prior administration had misused collection tools to unmask and surveil an incoming administration. Individuals from that administration had also leaked that information to the press, a serious crime. These were damning details in their own right, and House Intelligence Committee Democrats should have been appalled—given all their prior worries about the government violating civil liberties. Their decision to instead uniformly pile on Nunes shows the degree to which politics was driving their actions from the start.

Cue the coordinated effort to destroy Nunes. Almost immediately after his press conference, Democrats also began claiming that Nunes had broken the law. Oregon Senator Ron Wyden stated that because Nunes in his press conference had in passing mentioned FISA warrants, he had revealed "classified information." This was a crazy notion—Nunes didn't reveal anything about the warrants, and the press had already been rampantly speculating about FISA actions against the Trump campaign. It's also hardly a crime to say the word "FISA." But progressive groups allied with House Democrats immediately filed a volley of ethics complaints. The Republicans on the House Committee on Ethics caved in early April and announced the committee would formally initiate an investigation of Nunes for the "unauthorized disclosures of classified information." Nunes was forced to step aside from the panel's official probe into Russia's involvement in the 2016 election. Democrats, the media, and liberal Resistance groups had engineered false charges against a sitting congressman, smeared him for telling the truth, and removed him from a piece of the investigation—all to keep the truth from coming out. This was unprecedented, even in rough Washington.

Congressional ethics committees receive politically motivated complaints all the time, though they almost never act on them. That's because the members of those committees—right and left—have traditionally understood the danger of entertaining partisan petitions. Members have a self-interest in staying above the fray. Using the committee to pursue one party's members on purely political grounds opens the rival party's members to similar risks. So it says something that Democrats were willing to throw this understanding aside in their enthusiasm to get Nunes. The California Republican would later find out that four of the five committee Democrats had called for his removal from the Russia probe even before the ethics investigation into him was launched—a huge conflict for those who voted yes. And not only did they push for the probe, they then dragged it out as long as possible. Nunes immediately agreed to provide all the information the committee asked, and Republicans realized early there were no grounds to the Nunes accusation. But Democrats refused to close the examination, demanding more and more. It would take until December for the committee to clear Nunes, admitting there was never anything there. In the process, these Democrats violated all the traditional rules of one of few congressional bodies that—even in our partisan times—had retained a modicum of mutual respect and decorum.

* * *

Nunes didn't give up "all" of his investigation—which would prove crucial. Several of his Republican colleagues—Texas's Mike Conaway, South Carolina's Trey Gowdy, and Florida's Tom Rooney—took over the Russian-interference part. But Nunes, as House Intelligence Chairman, with oversight of the nation's surveillance laws, remained in control of a vital piece. He continued a narrowly focused probe into whether the Federal Bureau of Investigation had abused the FISA process.

That meant Nunes was able to ride herd on Fusion and Steele, the producers of the dossier that the FBI had used to obtain a FISA warrant on Carter Page. Since the dossier's public release in January, Republicans in the House and Senate had started to learn more concerning facts about that document and its authors. Former officials initially tried to put some distance between themselves and the corrupt dossier. Former Director of National Intelligence James Clapper, for instance, in the spring made a point of saying his people had never been able to "corroborate" the dossier's "sourcing."

Yet by early April 2016, the press had reported that the FBI had obtained a warrant on Page, and it was no leap to assume that application might have included information from the dossier. Republicans began to dig in, and Democrats again abused their positions to try to protect the tricksters.

An example of this scurrilous behavior came in July 2017,

when Senate Judiciary Chairman Chuck Grassley said he wanted to have both Trump Jr. and Manafort come and testify about the now-infamous Trump Tower meeting with that Russian lawyer, Veselnitskaya, in June 2016. Grassley had up to this point worked closely with his Democratic counterpart, Dianne Feinstein; the duo were known in D.C. for their ability to get along. And Democrats wanted nothing more than to put Trump Jr. and Manafort under the klieg lights. They insisted the hearing take place in public, for the world to hear. Grassley was up for it.

Then, suddenly, they backed off. They no longer wanted public testimony. Why? Because Grassley had demanded that Fusion GPS head Simpson also testify, and clearly some Democrats were terrified that the oppo-researcher would be asked under oath who had paid him to compile his dossier. They were willing to give up everything—including their Manafort Moment—just to protect Simpson.

Grassley meanwhile also wanted American-born businessman William Browder to testify. The Russian government in 2005 blacklisted Browder from the country, accusing him of engaging in financial corruption. Browder hired a Russian accountant, Sergei Magnitsky, who proved it was the opposite: The Russian government had engaged in rampant corruption and attempted to cover up the crimes. Magnitsky was arrested, beaten, and tortured; he later died in a Russian jail. The United States would ultimately pass the Magnitsky Act, signed by Obama, which punished via sanction those responsible for Magnitsky's death.

Veselnitskaya represented a Russian company accused by the U.S. government of money laundering, as part of the corruption uncovered by Magnitsky. Fusion had been hired by a U.S. law firm assisting Veselnitskaya to do a hit job on Browder, to undermine his claims. Grassley wanted Browder to explain the treatment meted out to him by the Fusion crowd—the slurs, the harassment, the ugly press stories. Democrats were so alarmed that their precious Simpson—owner of the dossier—might be called to account that they invoked a parliamentary maneuver just to temporarily keep Browder off the witness stand. Feinstein was so eager to protect Simpson that she was willing to destroy her long-standing relationship with Grassley and refused to sign his letter demanding that Simpson tell the committee who paid for the dossier.

Still, Republicans were getting an inkling of the dirty dossier trick. On July 28, 2017, the *WSJ* was the first to suggest that Hillary and the DNC were behind the document, based on solid information I'd received from sources. In a column titled "Who Paid for the Trump Dossier," I wrote: "Here's a thought: What if it was the Democratic National Committee or Hillary Clinton's campaign? What if that money flowed from a political entity on the left, to a private law firm, to Fusion, to a British spook, and then to Russian sources?" The left ridiculed that claim for months, but it was, in fact, exactly what happened. For so long, we'd heard the conspiracy theory that the Trump campaign had been colluding with Russians. It was backward. From the start, it was the Hillary campaign playing footsie with the Russians. Move aside the middlemen of Fusion and Steele and you ended up with this: The Democrats were paying dollars to collect Russian-provided accusations against Trump.

It would nonetheless take more than two months to establish that truth. As Nunes began to circle, Simpson retained Josh Levy as a lawyer. Levy wasn't just any attorney—he was a highly political, Democratic advocate. He formerly worked in Congress, as no less than counsel to Chuck Schumer—which says something about Fusion's ties. Nunes ultimately issued subpoenas for Fusion's bank records, which the company aggressively fought. Levy in October wrote a seventeen-page letter accusing Nunes of misdeeds and declaring his subpoenas invalid. He also refused to make Simpson available for testimony on the grounds that Fusion had a (hilarious) right to silence under the First Amendment.

The committee hauled Simpson in anyway, in what became a

circus of a private hearing. The Fusion team ultimately invoked the *Fifth* Amendment on everything—from its relationship to Steele, to the history of its work, to the role of the dossier. (Never mind the Fifth Amendment only protects you from providing self-incriminating evidence.) More revealing was the offensive behavior on the Democratic side. No Democratic members even bothered to come to the hearing. Instead, Democratic staffers took it upon themselves to shield Simpson from tough questions. At one point, staffers for ranking member Adam Schiff interrupted Republican Tom Rooney and accused him of badgering the witness and of acting inappropriately. This is not done; staffers do not interrupt congressmen. And they certainly don't accuse elected members of Congress of engaging in misbehavior or act as defense attorneys for witnesses. But the staffers did here. Again, it was an unprecedented moment and a crossing of lines. Why fight so hard to keep Simpson's secrets? Democrats clearly knew that the answers would be ugly.

Fusion would ultimately file a federal lawsuit to attempt to block the committee's subpoena of its bank records. But it never had a leg to stand on, and it ultimately folded. The committee's findings, in late October 2016, proved that Clinton and the DNC had paid for the dossier, via the law firm cutout of Perkins Coie. At least some journalists expressed outrage, claiming they had asked this question and been lied to. *NYT* reporter Kenneth Vogel tweeted: "When I tried to report this story, Clinton campaign lawyer [Marc Elias] pushed back vigorously, claiming 'You (or your sources) are wrong.'" Senior *NYT* White House correspondent Maggie Haberman added: "Folks involved in funding this lied about it, and with sanctimony, for a year." We will probably never know just how hard anyone in the mainstream media pressed for this story, if at all. But if Haberman is correct that the lawyers hid it for a year, the question is why that same mainstream media still treats him as a legitimate source. Which it does.

DNC officials immediately distanced themselves from the

news. The former DNC chair, Florida Representative Debbie Wasserman Schultz, who was in control at the time of the dossier commissioning, claimed to know nothing about it. So did her successor, Tom Perez. And a Perkins Coie spokesperson told the *Washington Post* that Elias "drew from funds he was authorized to spend without oversight from campaign officials." But lawyers told me they'd never heard of a law firm authorizing payments without the approval of the client. And notably the spokesperson did not outright deny that Elias told people in the DNC and Clinton sphere about the work.

Which meant a lot of people in Washington knew. Fusion delivered its product to its paymasters. It also filtered it through the State Department, the Justice Department, and the FBI. Comey in the spring of 2016 had briefed the Obama administration on his Trump-Russia concerns, and Brennan had briefed Senate minority leader Harry Reid. Just how many top Democrats knew about the dossier, pushed the FBI to act on it, and then worked to cover it up and sideline Republicans who started investigating? That we may never know. But this was the purest case in modern times of political actors co-opting the nation's intelligence and law enforcement agencies for political purpose, an unspeakable affront to free elections and liberty.

* * *

Fusion's obstruction was one thing; the Department of Justice's was another. From the moment Republicans understood that the FBI was investigating the Trump orbit, they began demanding information. And from that moment, the FBI and the DOJ resisted.

Consider the conflict of interest here, and the problem it presents for effective government oversight of U.S. spying agencies. The FBI—and/or U.S. intelligence agencies—engages in behavior that is inappropriate and at odds with the laws Congress has passed. It knows this and does not want Congress to find out. It has, in fact, specifically conjured up a "counterintelligence investigation" to further shroud its probe in secrecy. When Congress demands information about the investigation, it pleads "sources and methods" and "classified information" and the "integrity of investigations" as excuses to stonewall requests. These are the very privileges Congress has granted intelligence agencies, now being used to keep Congress from rooting out bad behavior.

The Justice Department's refusal to comply with House and Senate requests was more disturbing than even that. Congress has what's known as the "Gang of Eight," a group of senior leaders of the legislature who are routinely briefed on classified intelligence by the executive branch. They include the leaders of each of the two parties in the Senate and the House, and the chairs and ranking members of those bodies' intelligence committees. The Gang of Eight has always been made privy to the United States' most sensitive intelligence operations, including for instance, George W. Bush's enhanced interrogation program.

In a *WSJ* op-ed published in May 2018, a 33-year veteran of the FBI described his own experience working with Congress. Thomas J. Baker served as a special agent and legal attaché. As he wrote: "Former Directors William Webster (1978-87) and Louis Freeh (1993-2001) insisted that the FBI respond promptly to any congressional request. In those days a congressional committee didn't need a subpoena to get information from the FBI." He explained: "My colleagues and I shared the general sense that responding to congressional requests was the right thing to do. The bureau's leaders often reminded us of Congress's legitimate oversight role. This was particularly true of the so-called Gang of Eight, which was created by statute to ensure the existence of a secure vehicle through which congressional leaders could be briefed on the most sensitive counterintelligence or terrorism investigations." Baker went on to say that the Bureau's refusal to supply information in the Russia case was nothing less than "shocking." He was appalled that Comey had not briefed Congress on the Trump-Russia affair, and that the FBI was refusing other requests. "The Gang of Eight exists for precisely this purpose," he wrote. "Not using it is inexplicable." Baker's piece put in context the FBI's behavior; its refusal to provide Congress information was a disturbing first, another result of the Resistance.

Indeed, for six long months the DOJ resolutely refused to provide Nunes, Grassley, and others with the most basic of information. The man technically leading this obstruction was Deputy AG Rosenstein, and two facts about him explain the change in the sharing culture under his tenure. The first: Rosenstein had spent his life within the DOJ orbit. By the time he'd been confirmed deputy attorney general in April 2017, he'd ranked as the nation's longest-serving U.S. attorney. Rosenstein was the ultimate institutionalist, committed to protecting his lifelong employer. The second: Rosenstein's own name was on the bottom of one of the final Page FISA renewal applications in the summer of 2017. He'd been involved in at least part of the Russia inquiry, had worked with McCabe in launching the Trump probe, and had a personal interest in keeping things under wraps.

The biggest battle came over documents that Nunes had every right to see. The Intelligence chairman had taken care to keep his probe narrowly focused on issues that pertained directly to the FISA laws that his committee helps oversee; he was acting in a true oversight capacity. He wasn't asking for paper covered under executive privilege, and his specific requests made clear he was not on a fishing expedition. He also had clearance to see the most classified documents on the planet.

Nunes spent his first months politely requesting documents, only to be ignored. This prompted his first round of subpoenas, sent on August 24, 2017. Even seasoned members, who were used to interbranch tussles, were floored when the DOJ flatly refused to comply. DOJ and FBI representatives splayed a litany of excuses, every one more ridiculous than the next. They claimed that providing documents might undermine the "integrity" of the

Mueller probe—as if special counsel and congressional investigations couldn't proceed apace. If the goal was truly answers, the more the investigators, the better. They claimed it was too dangerous to provide classified material, as this might undermine sources and methods. But members like Nunes had been looking at just that sort of material for years. They claimed that cooperation might interfere with a separate probe by the Justice Department inspector general. This was the most ludicrous of all. Congress *created* inspector generals, and in no situation do those internal watchdogs trump legitimate oversight by the legislative branch.

When Republicans called these bluffs, the DOJ instead turned to delay and misdirection. Nunes was invited in to be briefed by an FBI official—but was ultimately provided nothing of value. FBI Director Christopher Wray sat before the House Judiciary Committee in December and engaged in an epic five hours of stonewalling. He continued to hold out the inspector general probe as his excuse not to answer any questions. His spinning was so over the top that it at times bordered on absurd. Wray at one point claimed that he did not believe he could "legally and appropriately share a FISA court submission" with the committee, since such documents were "all covered with a 'classified information' cover." As if members of Congress don't have classified clearance, and as if the Judiciary Committee doesn't have the right to look at the work product of a FISA court system it helped create.

In the Senate, the DOJ similarly refused to cooperate with document demands from Johnson and Grassley, even ignoring bipartisan requests. The department also refused to make available witnesses, again on the grounds that to do so would undermine other probes. In early December, the Mueller team acknowledged that Peter Strzok, one of the lead investigators on Trump-Russia, had been abruptly removed from the special counsel's team after the DOJ inspector general discovered a tranche of highly partisan text messages he'd exchanged with his lover, FBI lawyer Lisa Page. The first of those texts became public about a week later, showing Strzok and Page variously referring to Trump during 2016 as an "idiot" and "loathsome" (to name a few), while also expressing their clear preference for a Clinton presidency. The duo at one point discussed an "insurance policy" in the unlikely event Trump were elected. Despite this explosive new information, the DOJ would not make Strzok or Page or other key witnesses available for interviews.

Nunes finally threatened to bring contempt charges against Rosenstein and Wray and gave a deadline of January 3, 2018. The DOJ at that point pulled a stunt for the ages. Throughout this entire fight, Republicans had been learning about and focusing more on the dossier. They'd discovered in the fall that Democrats had funded it and were highly suspicious it had played a major role in the FBI's investigation. Many of the documents the House demanded were, in fact, dossier-related. Not long after Nunes issued his contempt threat, anonymous sources leaked that infamous "origin" story to the *New York Times*. The piece claimed the entire investigation had been prompted by Papadopoulos and explicitly demoted the dossier's role. The very next day, the *Washington Post* ran a separate hit piece on Nunes, claiming, again with anonymous sources, that his Republican colleagues had lost confidence in him. "So a leak about how the dossier doesn't matter after all, and another saying I'm out there alone," Nunes recounted to me later. "And right then [Rosenstein] and [Wray] suddenly demand a private meeting with [Speaker Paul Ryan], where they try to convince him to make me stand down. All of this is not a coincidence." Ryan, to his credit, didn't fall for the brazen ruse and backed up Nunes's demands. A few hours later, Nunes was able to announce that the DOJ had agreed to let committee investigators *finally* see the material they demanded.

Washington is a dirty place, but this episode was more disturbing than most. The Justice Department and the FBI hold awesome powers. In the days of J. Edgar Hoover, they abused their information-collecting capacities by maintaining files on members of Congress—to keep people in line. While the targeting of Nunes wasn't quite that slimy, it should worry every American that prosecutors and law enforcement officials are willing to smear elected legislators—just to hide their secrets. The *Washington Post* and *New York Times* stories once again sent the message to the federal bureaucracy that leaks and slurs are an acceptable—even routine—part of government business. They are not.

The months of obstruction also did serious long-term damage to Congress's oversight authority. Fights over executive privilege are nothing new. Nixon invoked executive privilege to protect himself during Watergate. Clinton invoked it more than a dozen times, in part to bar Ken Starr from questioning some of his aides. George W. Bush invoked it with regard to questions about the firing of U.S. attorneys. Obama invoked it to protect information about his botched Fast & Furious gunrunning operation.

But nobody in 2017 ever deigned to suggest the DOJ documents in question were subject to executive privilege. Quite the opposite. This was information—as former FBI legal attaché Baker noted in his op-ed—that Congress had been free to view in the past. That's because those documents fell squarely under congressional oversight, and moreover the sharing between the congressional and the legislative branches of counterintelligence information is important for national security.

Yet the DOJ's unprecedented refusal to share exposed just how few powers Congress has to compel a mulish department to comply. Rosenstein and Wray ultimately chose to avoid contempt resolutions—but only after months of delay. And even if Congress had issued those resolutions, the DOJ would likely have refused to act on them, forcing Congress to engage in years of litigation. Future executive branch departments now understand that there are few immediate consequences to balking congressional subpoenas. That will only embolden bureaucrats to overstep, in the knowledge that they have the ability to keep their actions hidden in the longer term.

* * *

Nunes and his compatriots were finally off to view key dossier documents. In the same week, Grassley and Lindsey Graham sent to the DOJ a criminal referral against Steele. They'd discovered enough to believe that Steele had lied to the FBI about his interactions with the media. Congressional Democrats went into a panic and again ramped up. They proved willing to wreck more committee reputations and rules in their rush to deflect from what Republicans were finding.

Feinstein almost immediately took the extraordinary step of unilaterally releasing the transcript of Simpson's Senate Judiciary Committee testimony from the prior August. It was an extraordinary break with procedure and a hard-nosed snub of Grassley, who had worked collegially with her for years.

The clear intent of the release was to get out ahead of Republican findings and rehabilitate the dossier. Simpson's transcript presented Steele in a fawning light, a "Boy Scout," with "quality" intelligence-gathering skills, a man nobly interested in saving the United States from Putin—rather than a gun-for-hire. Feinstein was aided directly in her campaign by Simpson and his co-founder, Peter Fritsch, who in early January ran an op-ed in the *New York Times*, in which they lauded their own dossier work, claiming their only interest had been to "highlight Mr. Trump's Russia ties." Their line: All that mattered were the motives and credentials of Steele, and he was great. They did not include the fact that the noble Steele had blabbed to the press and been dismissed by the FBI. And remember, all this came out at exactly the moment it became clear Nunes would be getting the truth about the degree to which the FBI had used the dossier. Since Ms. Feinstein's unilateral release, members all over Congress (including Republicans) have felt at liberty to unilaterally release documents. Another line erased. Thank you, Resistance.

Ms. Feinstein's behavior was matched only by that of her

ranking colleague on the Senate Intelligence Committee, Virginia's Mark Warner. Having successfully mau-maued Chairman Richard Burr into working "cooperatively" with Democrats, Mr. Warner set about running the show. It would later come out that in March 2017, Warner began secretly texting with a lobbyist who offered to put him in touch with Steele. Warner didn't tell his committee colleagues about this for months. He instead insisted in his messages that he alone on the committee should talk to Steele first, about the "scope" of any possible testimony. That didn't come to pass, but why was Warner so worried about what Steele might say?

Warner's bigger achievement was to keep the Senate investigation going and going and going—allowing him to continue spinning collusion theories, even as the committee provided no answers. Most of the other committees digging into the Russia question were producing reams of important information. Grassley and Nunes had dug into Fusion, the dossier, Steele, the FISA warrants. Johnson had investigated leaks and pushed the release of vital Strzok-Page text messages. The Burr-Warner investigation? A black hole. As the *WSJ* wrote in an October 2017 editorial: "As the Republican Chairman of the Senate Intelligence Committee and the Democratic Ranking Member held a press conference Wednesday about their investigation into Russia's role in the 2016 presidential election, a nearby sign highlighted their effort: 11 open hearings, 100-plus people interviewed, 4,000 transcript pages and 100,000 pages of documents." Answers: none.

The embarrassing part was Republican committee members' willingness to endure this political mugging. Whereas Schiff had destroyed committee comity, Warner successfully used it against his GOP colleagues. "Bipartisanship" in Warner's dictionary meant that committee Democrats got to make unfounded accusations against Trump and his team, while Republicans were required to sit silently by—lest they be accused of uncongeniality.

Warner was helped in this effort by a press corps that continued to gush over just how professionally the committee was working.

Burr even allowed his fiefdom to be turned into something akin to the terrifying House Un-American Activities Committee, which pursued putative communists. Burr's committee began sending letters to absolutely everyone about their Russian acquaintances. They sent one to Robert Barnes, an attorney for Charles C. Johnson, a controversial alt-right blogger. The letter demanded he turn over "any communications with Russian persons." The attorney queried just what this meant. Russians in Russia? Russians in America? Russians who may have engaged in the election? Russians who might be interested in politics? The committee's response was more chilling than even Barnes might have imagined. It wrote that its letter "may be read to refer to persons that Mr. Johnson knows or has reason to believe that are of Russian nationality or *descent*" (emphasis added). Consider that phrase, and imagine replacing the words with persons of "Arab or Arab descent."

Over in the House, South Carolina's Trey Gowdy would point out that the Democrats' desired "witness list" was so expansive that it read like "pretty much every character in any Dostoevsky or Tolstoy novel." There are at least 130 million Russians on the planet, and only a few dozen had anything to do with the 2016 election. Yet here were senators suggesting that the mere act of knowing someone with a Russian last name was potentially treasonous. Burr's committee came far closer to breaching that civil liberties line than anything Trump was ever accused of, and nobody in the D.C. press corps cared one bit.

Yet none of this held a candle to the behavior of California Representative Adam Schiff, who managed in a few short months to destroy the reputation of one of the last grown-up committees in Congress. For decades, the House and Senate Intelligence Committees had held themselves out as a redoubt of reasonableness and bipartisanship. Only serious members tended to ask to serve in these hard posts, and only serious members tended to be named. Committee members prided themselves on putting national security ahead of partisan politics and generally refusing to undercut one another.

Schiff, the ranking member under Nunes, officially ended all that. When Nunes exposed the information about Obama administration unmaskings, Schiff chose to berate the Republican rather than treat the information seriously. This was startlingly partisan, given that for years Democrats had made an issue about government spying, privacy, and civil liberties. The left had blown a gasket over the Republican authorization of metadata, which merely allows the government to collect telephone numbers—no names, and no eavesdropping. And Oregon Senator Ron Wyden in 2013 had introduced a bill to strengthen the ban on reverse targeting, for fear the government would use surveillance of foreign citizens to listen in on Americans. Yet now with clear proof that the Obama administration had abused its unmasking authority, Schiff moved to shoot the messenger.

He followed this up with a jaw-dropping performance on March 20, 2017, in which he used a House Intelligence Committee hearing to present the crazy dossier allegations as fact. It was nothing less than shocking to watch one of the higher-ranking members of Congress, sitting on one of the more responsible committees, spew libelous, unverified accusations of treason in a public hearing. Two days later, Schiff would launch a full-blown national hysteria when he claimed on NBC's *Meet the Press Daily* that the Intelligence Committee already had "more than circumstantial evidence" that the Trump campaign had colluded with Russia. Washington does not suffer from a lack of irresponsible statements, but Schiff's were singular.

An even more dishonorable moment came nearly a year later, in February 2018. The entire House Intelligence Committee had finally been allowed to see pertinent FISA documents, and Nunes now knew for certain that the FBI had used the dossier as a central part of its FISA application against Page, that the FBI hadn't been straight with the court about Steele and his political masters, and that the FBI had recycled a news story to the court. Republicans put together a "memo" describing these and other alarming findings. This was everything Democrats had feared.

Their initial response was to fight tooth and nail against its public release. When this looked likely to fail, Schiff instead produced a "rival" memo. His document would later prove to be a bald misrepresentation of the facts. It claimed that "FBI and DOJ officials did not 'abuse' the [FISA] process, omit material information, or subvert this vital tool to spy on the Trump campaign." Untrue. But at the time nobody other than the committee had seen the FISA documents, and the press was happy to run with Schiff's assessment. The Nunes memo was important and ultimately sparked Sessions to formally ask the DOJ inspector general to conduct an investigation into whether the FBI had abused the FISA process. And when the DOJ that summer finally released redacted versions of the Page FISA applications, Nunes's memo was utterly vindicated. But Schiff had managed to once again keep the collusion narrative flowing.

Schiff would continue this unprofessional behavior—even through the Mueller report. He fought Nunes on releasing a full committee report on findings, he continued to claim he had "evidence" of Trump collusion, and his side of the committee continued to leak information designed to undermine their Republican colleagues. I at one point sent an e-mail to Schiff's office asking for an on-the-record response to just when, exactly, Schiff first knew about the dossier and the fact that Democrats had paid for it. I never received a response.

* * *

Meanwhile, the Justice Department wasn't yet done trying to hide information. Nunes and others had managed to see the crucial FISA documents and put out their memo. At the end of March 2018, committee Republicans announced they had finished their investigation and had readied a final report on Russia's interference in 2016, along with recommendations to prevent a repeat. The committee had engaged in an exhaustive probe, one that proved spot on. It managed to conclude a full year before Mueller that there was no Trump-Russia collusion and to spotlight Russia's damaging efforts in the election.

The report nonetheless also contained damaging information about the FBI's actions in 2016, and the DOJ instantly claimed the right to redact it. When the DOJ finally allowed a heavily blacked out report to emerge nearly a month later, Republicans were furious by what the department had hidden. The DOJ has a clear and legitimate interest in redacting information that could hurt national security. But the GOP quickly realized that the DOJ and FBI had also redacted information solely to spare the FBI from embarrassment. Just one example: Footnote 43 of the intelligence report explained that the then–FBI general counsel, Jim Baker, met in the fall of 2016 with a person who had provided information about Trump-Russia links. The person's name was blacked out. We'd find out much later that it was, of course, the Perkins Coie lawyer who worked for the Clinton campaign: Michael Sussmann. National security concerns? Hardly.

Grassley in the Senate was struggling with the same problem. By May 2018, he'd not been allowed to question a single current or former DOJ or FBI official involved in the affair. More than a year into his demand for the transcript of former National Security Advisor Michael Flynn's call with the Russian ambassador, he'd still not received it—nor any of the reports from the FBI agents who'd interviewed Flynn. Grassley excoriated the DOJ for redacting key information from the documents they had provided and for refusing to provide a "privilege log"—which details the legal basis for withholding information. He was especially incensed after he found out that one of the items the DOJ had scrubbed from the Strzok-Page texts was a message about the duo's concern over the cost of former Deputy FBI Director Andrew McCabe's conference table. It had cost $70,000. That the FBI blew more money on one piece of furniture than many Americans earn in a year is a scandal—not a matter of national security.

But the low in the DOJ's behavior came in the spring, when House Republicans sniffed out evidence that the FBI had done far more than just use electronic surveillance against the Trump campaign—it had also run an informant. The truly stunning part of this tale was the lengths to which the DOJ went to hide this information from Congress. The subpoenas Nunes had issued way back in August clearly encompassed this information—yet the FBI concealed the facts. The only way it could have done so was to scrub other documents, in a deliberate effort to make sure the House didn't get wind of its informant. Speaker Paul Ryan emphasized this point in May 2018, when he stated that Nunes's demand for this information was "wholly appropriate" and "completely within the scope" of the committee's investigation" and "something that probably should have been answered a while ago."

Yet Rosenstein's response to the demand for more information was to double down and to publicly accuse the committee of "extortion"—an inflammatory comment. The DOJ used every conceivable excuse to try to get around giving House leaders the details. It delayed. It claimed that answering Nunes's request could result in the "loss of human life." It pleaded with the White House to intervene on its behalf.

In May, we at the *WSJ*, via our own reporting, realized there had been an informant. I'm proud to say we were the first to report that the FBI had used an asset—a "top secret intelligence source"—to spy on members of the Trump campaign. I'm also proud to say that we independently figured out the name of the informant—Stefan Halper. No member of Congress ever gave

it to us or confirmed it. We chose not to run it out of concerns for national security. We were also worried by reports to us
that the DOJ was raring to open criminal leak investigations into
Republican members—not because those members had actually
leaked anything, but in retribution for their efforts to find information. We didn't want to provide a pretext.

We needn't have bothered with our caution. My column about
the informant appeared on May 11, 2018. Within weeks, anonymous "current and former government officials" had leaked
everything about the "informant" and his work to the *New York
Times* and the *Washington Post*. The leaks were clearly designed to
present the FBI's actions in the most favorable light. The *NYT*
headline actually read (no joke): "FBI Used Informant to Investigate Russia Ties to Campaign, Not to Spy, as Trump Claims." The
stories didn't specifically use Halper's name but spilled everything else: his profession, where he lived, whom he'd talked to
on the Trump campaign, the dates of those interactions. It was a
roadmap to Halper, and soon his name was all over the press.

In short, someone blew a source, just to ensure the FBI and
the DOJ had a better storyline. People connected to the Justice
Department and the FBI were happy to release information to
their media Boswells, even as they threatened elected members of
Congress. Nunes would later make an astute observation. Asked
why he'd gone to all the effort he had, he responded: "A lot of
the bad and problematic countries . . . this is what they do there.
There is a political party that controls the intelligence agencies,
controls the media, all to ensure that party stays in power. If we
get to that here, we no longer have a functioning republic. We
can't let that happen."

Indeed. In college, I was a student of Russian affairs. And
the twin sides of this episode—threats against those who might
speak out alongside spoon-fed media narratives—reminded me
of something: *Pravda*.

Ironic, right?

The DOJ and the FBI continued their obstruction right through the 2018 election. Their slow rolling looked deliberately designed to wait out Republicans, hoping Democrats would take over the House and drop the probe. Nunes, upon finishing his Intelligence Committee investigation, passed along a list of some forty names of witnesses to Judiciary Chairman Goodlatte and Oversight Chairman Gowdy—who were continuing their own work. The DOJ hemmed and hawed about making people available. By the time Democrats took over in 2019, Goodlatte and Gowdy had made it through only a portion of their list. And Democrats instantly announced an end to any more investigation.

* * *

One further change in Washington has proven corrosive to our body politic: Our former intelligence chiefs will not go away. In January 2017, the newly elected leader of the Senate Democrats, Chuck Schumer, made a statement that even some in his own party found chilling. Schumer chided Trump for rapping law enforcement and spies. "Let me tell you," he said on MSNBC's *Rachel Maddow Show*. "You take on the intelligence community— they have six ways from Sunday at getting back at you."

It is generally unheard of for former FBI or CIA or national intelligence directors to continue to insert themselves in the political realm. But Comey, Clapper, and Brennan have become national partisan commentators, playing a key role in spinning up the collusion narrative. After the leak of his memos, the Senate Judiciary Committee sent Comey a letter asking him a series of questions: Did he have other memos? Whom had he shared them with? Did he retain copies? Comey responded that he didn't have to answer any of these questions because he was now a "private citizen." The private citizen nonetheless agreed to serve as star public performer at a Senate Intelligence Committee hearing in June 2017.

In advance, the committee released his long and detailed testimony about his interactions with Trump, in which he painted the president in the worst possible light. He used the hearing to have it both ways: to leave the impression that Trump had committed a crime, even as he refused to answer questions about any details or his own failure as a senior law enforcement official to report or deter the supposed misconduct. He also, of course, wrote and published his book in 2018 and went on an extended tour in which he twisted the facts to his favor at every opportunity. Brennan took a job as an "analyst" at NBC News; Clapper took one at CNN. Both freely smacked Trump on every occasion, offering their theories as to why he was clearly guilty of collusion. Because of their former roles, these opinions were given outsized weight.

In late 2018, the quarterly *International Journal of Intelligence and Counterintelligence* ran a lengthy piece from twelve-year CIA analyst John Gentry, who criticized Brennan and former CIA Director Michael Morell for breaking a long-standing prohibition against airing political views. He noted that "for senior former intelligence officials to make such blatantly partisan statements is unprecedented." He took aim at Morell's 2016 *NYT* op-ed that advocated for Clinton as president. "Morell's claim that his CIA career qualifies him to make political judgments about domestic issues is incorrect," wrote Gentry. "He was trained and authorized to 'make the call' about foreign intelligence issues within the classified, internal world of the U.S. government." Comey's self-aggrandizing claims that he possessed some special claim on loyalty or dignity are equally without foundation. Nothing in the FBI director's work or history gave him some special claim on virtue. Quite the opposite; he proved himself as ruthless a Washington player as they come. It is unclear why the press continues to turn to him—or Brennan or Clapper—as a source of unbiased "analysis."

In the end, all the obstruction, the grandstanding, and the

smear campaigns were largely for naught. The important information about the dossier, its funders, and the FBI's use of the document came out. We'll get even more details now that Attorney General Bill Barr has tasked U.S. Attorney John Durham with investigating the investigators. But the antics will have enduring consequences. The obstruction exposed Congress's inability to enforce subpoenas, and Pelosi Democrats are already finding it harder to obtain information. Congressional committees that we have long depended on to keep us safe (the House Intelligence Committee) or to keep members in line (the House Ethics Committee) are now riven with distrust. And the Comey-Brennan-Clapper Show has made Americans even more skeptical of the neutrality and professionalism of our law enforcement and intelligence organizations. The Resistance campaign to hide the truth—to keep the collusion narrative rolling and take out Trump—further broke critical pieces of the executive and the legislative branches.

And yet they kept it up to the bitter end — even beyond. Well past the time it was clear that even Mueller would not be able to establish collusion, the haters kept pushing the collusion narrative. Even at the end of 2018, Democrats were still demanding Republicans pass legislation to "protect" Mueller's probe. They kept holding out hope that Mueller would finally deliver a report that would allow them to nullify the 2016 election. But all the hope in the world could not change the facts: that this had never been anything more than the co-option of our democratic institutions to smear a political opponent.

CHAPTER 6

A MUELLER SPECIAL

Special counsels are among the most corrosive institutions in U.S. democracy. It's a headline-driven and glory-filled job, which attracts the worst legal prima donnas. It's an astonishingly powerful job, which encourages prosecutors to stretch the boundaries of the law. It's also a job nearly bereft of political accountability. Once you appoint a special counsel, there is no disciplining or stopping them.

Bob Mueller exemplified all these problems. By the end of his two-year investigation into Trump-Russia collusion, he'd left a tornado trail of hardball tactics, ugly prosecutions, empty bank accounts, and demolished reputations. What he never brought was a single indictment related to the subject he'd been asked to investigate: collusion. His handpicked team of Clinton partisans sowed further distrust in Justice Department operations. And far from closing the book on the Trump-Russia controversy, Mueller's final, highly political report further divided Washington and the country.

Mueller spent 675 days and more than $25 million to fail. The important prosecutions he brought—against the Russians who interfered in the 2016 elections—could just as easily have been brought by regular law enforcement. And many of the Americans he jailed were prosecuted for their interactions with the special prosecutor himself; they'd have never happened if not for the Mueller probe. If there's any upside to this spectacle, it's the hope that Washington never appoints another special counsel again.

* * *

Republicans were right to spend so much of early 2017 opposing Democratic calls for a special counsel. Nothing good has ever come of those posts. Exhibit A: Comey's appointment in 2003 of his good buddy U.S. Attorney Patrick Fitzgerald to investigate who leaked CIA agent Valerie Plame's name to the press. Fitzgerald discovered early on that the leak had come from then–Deputy Secretary of State Richard Armitage. Rather than close up shop, he pursued flimsy obstruction charges against Vice President Dick Cheney's chief of staff, Scooter Libby. Fitzgerald let the country incorrectly believe for two years that a crime may have been committed by people close to the president and the vice president.

Republicans also understood the Democrats' ultimate goal: to prosecute their way to the presidency. Americans elected Trump in 2016, but the haters refused to accept the results. Democrats, too, knew the history of special counsels and reckoned another one was their best shot at erecting a legal case against Trump, either paving the way for impeachment or easing their path to the White House in 2020.

But the GOP's capitulation on a special counsel in the spring of 2017 held consequences far beyond the Trump presidency—it opened the door to more abuse of core institutions as well as the erosion of constitutional powers.

Mueller's appointment stretched the boundaries of the DOJ's special-counsel regulations, making that position even more threatening in the future. Rosenstein made a serious error with his appointment letter: He didn't task Mueller with investigating a specific crime. His order instead charged Mueller with investigating "any links and/or coordination between the Russian government and individuals associated with the campaign of President Donald J. Trump," as well as "any matters that arose or may arise directly from the investigation." It was the first time a special counsel had been handed a broad counterintelligence investigation, and it allowed Mueller to probe anyone or anything even vaguely associated with the Trump campaign, for any reason. Special counsels are already supremely powerful. This unclear assignment guaranteed the Mueller probe would be longer and more intrusive than most, and would create an unnerving precedent for the future.

The ambiguity meanwhile allowed Mueller to brazenly pick up and run with the Comey-McCabe obstruction claim. At the time of the appointment, Comey had already leaked his memos and launched his obstruction narrative. If Rosenstein had wanted Mueller to look into obstruction, he'd have spelled that out. He deliberately did not include it in his appointment letter. Mueller used his fuzzy marching orders as his excuse to proceed anyway.

And the Comey-Mueller obstruction claim carried debilitating consequences for the office of the presidency. Presidents who exercise their legitimate powers of office cannot be accused of obstructing justice. Among those core powers are the right to direct law enforcement and to fire appointees. Trump might have erred in firing Comey at the precise time he did, but there is no question he had the right to make the error. If Congress believes a president has abused his powers, the Constitution provides it with a remedy: the power to impeach. But neither Comey nor Mueller had any business criminalizing the president's exercise of his office.

Their decision to do so undermined the separation of powers and put Trump in an untenable position throughout the Mueller probe. The haters whipped out the argument to oppose *other* legitimate presidential actions. Trump foes claimed that any use of his presidential pardon power would amount to obstruction. They claimed that his personal naming of a Comey successor would amount to obstruction. When Trump ordered his Justice Department to comply with congressional document demands, his critics claimed he was . . . obstructing (the special counsel probe). When Trump pointed out his power to fire Mueller for conflicts of interest, we were told that, too, would amount to obstruction—even though Trump absolutely has the power to terminate a special counsel, and even though the investigation would have continued under a Mueller replacement. Future presidents are now at risk of similar arguments against their constitutional powers.

The other major consequence of the Mueller appointment: It forestalled for two years public accountability for those who had engaged in FBI and DOJ conduct. It froze other oversight. The Justice Department used the Mueller probe as its excuse to deny Congress documents and witnesses, claiming that to do so would interfere with the special counsel's work. The Mueller probe similarly put the White House in a straitjacket; it could not declassify information or order an internal DOJ investigation, for fear of being accused of "obstructing" the special counsel. The American public was denied for two years vital information about government's actions in 2016, but instead was fed an endless stream of media accusation and speculation. It was corrosive to the country and undermined faith in government. As a *Wall Street Journal* editorial warned in March 2017: A special counsel probe would serve as a black hole, allowing Democrats to "claim for months or years that the 2016 election was stolen even if no indictments were ever handed up." Which is exactly what happened.

* * *

Appointing a special counsel was Rosenstein's first mistake; appointing Bob Mueller specifically was his second. While the press and Democrats lauded the former FBI director to no end, Mueller was always the wrong man for the job.

Why? The medical profession lives by a lot of rules, but a big one is that it is generally a bad idea for doctors to treat their friends or relatives. No matter how skilled or how ethical the doctor, he risks losing his objectivity when he treats loved ones. Even by the time of Mueller's appointment, it was clear the FBI had played a starring role in the Trump-Russia collusion story. Mueller never had the objectivity to evaluate the institution he used to run.

Mueller was a Princeton grad and a decorated Marine—as his supporters never stopped reminding people. Yet most of his life had been spent as a federal prosecutor, in senior positions at the Justice Department, and as the twelve-year director of the FBI. Federal prosecutors are a band of brothers—a legal elite. They aren't much for outside criticism, and they don't generally take shots at each other. The FBI is even more insular, its senior leaders blindly committed to protecting its reputation and its secrets. The only person who ever ran the FBI longer than Mueller was Hoover himself.

Mueller was also close to Comey. A Mueller biographer would write in *Politico* that Comey "treated Mueller as a close friend and almost mentor." The two had worked together, and had even—back in that famous 2004 episode—threatened to resign together from the Bush administration over a surveillance program. Mueller was the last person to sit in judgment of Trump, the man who'd fired his friend and fellow former FBI head.

Mueller proved that almost immediately when he chose his team—a disconcertingly stacked group of Clinton supporters, some of whom had also been central to the FBI and DOJ's poor decision making in 2016. As even the *Washington Post* would acknowledge in an article in March 2018, thirteen of the seventeen members of Mueller's team had previously registered as Democrats. Nine of them had "made political donations to Democrats," and six had donated directly to Hillary Clinton.

Mueller's deputy, Andrew Weissmann—dubbed his "pit bull"—
had attended Clinton's election night party in 2016. Weissmann,
who'd been a top DOJ lawyer, also had clearly been one of those
aware of the dossier. Ohr testified that Weissmann was among
those he warned in the summer of 2016 of Steele's bias against
Trump.

Most of Mueller's team was, in fact, made up of Justice
Department veterans who lacked the critical distance to conduct
a fair probe—Zainab Ahmad, Brandon Van Grack, Greg Andres,
Andrew Goldstein, to name a few. Elizabeth Prelogar had clerked
for two of the Supreme Court's more liberal justices—Ruth
Bader Ginsburg and Elena Kagan. And Mueller brought in
Jeannie Rhee, who'd served in Obama's Office of Legal Counsel.

The special counsel would also, infamously, hire Peter Strzok,
and one of Mueller's worst decisions was to do nothing more than
remove him from the team when he found out about Strzok's partisan texts. Getting rid of Strzok was not a fix. The revelation of
bias by Strzok and others, as the DOJ inspector general would
later explain, "cast a cloud over the investigations to which these
employees were assigned." And that cloud transferred to the
Mueller probe, injecting into it what the legal world calls the
"fruit of the poisonous tree."

As lawyers David Rivkin and Elizabeth Price Foley would write
in the *WSJ*: "If [the Trump-Russia collusion investigation] was
politically motivated, then its culmination, the appointment of
a special counsel, inherited the taint. All special-counsel
activities—investigations, plea deals, subpoenas, reports, indictment and convictions—are fruit of a poisonous tree, byproducts
of a violation of due process. That Mr. Mueller and his staff had
nothing to do with [that investigation's origin] offers no cure."
Due process, they explained, is most certainly violated by any
"prosecutorial efforts that appear, under the totality of circumstances, to be motivated by corruption, bias or entrapment." In
short, when Mueller discovered those Strzok texts, the answer

wasn't to fire him; it was to pause the probe until someone analyzed the FBI's behavior in 2016. He didn't. Instead, he withheld the information about Strzok's partisan bias, and his removal, from Congress.

Mueller's unsuitability grew startlingly clear in October 2017, when Nunes confirmed that the Clinton campaign and DNC had paid for the dossier. The FBI had been caught in the act of pursuing evidence against Trump that had been supplied by his presidential rival. Any fair investigation would obviously need to dig into the FBI's actions, and as former FBI head, Mueller had a blatant conflict of interest. The *WSJ* editorial page called for Mueller to resign. Our editorial was met with hysterical condemnation by Democrats and the media, suggesting we'd joined a campaign to cover up Trump's "crimes." This was ridiculous, given we'd called for the probe to go on—just under the leadership of someone more suited to step back and look at the totality of 2016's events. But the haters had placed their own bet on Mueller; they also knew his history and ties, and figured he'd take it to Trump and ignore the FBI's role. They continued to laud Mueller as a "straight arrow," but his report would show they'd made a wise bet: Mueller began from the premise that Comey and his FBI could do no wrong.

* * *

From his appointment in May 2017 to October of that year, Mueller's probe was a locked box, leading to wild press speculation. But this was nothing compared to the media frenzy that accompanied his first indictments.

Mueller's prosecutions fell into three categories. The first were those charges that had absolutely nothing to do with his remit. The special counsel justified these on the grounds that he had a duty to pursue any crime he came across. Yet as will be noted later, Mueller was more than happy to close his eyes to crimes squarely in front of him. The real goal of these prosecutions was to squeeze his targets, to threaten them with a lifetime in jail if they did not produce "the goods" on the Trump team.

A case study was Mueller's prosecution of Paul Manafort. Prior to joining the Trump campaign team in the spring of 2016, Manafort spent decades as the classic Beltway bandit—running a lucrative lobbying business. Mueller on October 30 would indict Manafort and his business partner Rick Gates on twelve counts including money laundering, failure to report foreign banking accounts, and conspiracy against the United States. The charges related entirely to work Manafort had done for pro-Russian Ukrainian politicians long before he'd joined the Trump campaign.

Unfortunately for Manafort and Gates, they had no "goods" to give Mueller—as we now know. Yet, to increase the pressure, Mueller in February 2018 filed a further thirty-two financial charges against the two men. Gates crumpled the next day, pleading guilty to conspiracy and lying to investigators. Manafort continued to fight the charges, for which he was punished by Mueller's team by being kept in solitary confinement for twenty-three hours a day. It was extraordinarily harsh treatment for a man who had been charged with nonviolent offenses.

Mueller's fervor to get his targets held severe consequences for more than Manafort; it was corrosive to the justice system. Among other things, the special counsel charged Manafort with violating the Foreign Agents Registration Act. FARA is a dusty 1938 statute that requires "agents" of a foreign government or principals to disclose their activities. In fifty years through 2016, the Justice Department brought only seven criminal FARA cases and won three convictions. Two were dismissed and two others pleaded to non-FARA charges. Beltway operators had without doubt been playing fast and loose with the law, but that was in part because the DOJ's infrequent enforcement had led to confusion about when FARA applied. DOJ had never bothered to explain publicly—either through regulations or guidance—what conduct is or isn't FARA-compliant. And the entire Washington lobbying world had long operated with the understanding that FARA violations would be dealt with administratively. When the DOJ occasionally called someone out for FARA, the parties sat down to work out a settlement—usually retroactive registration and a fine.

Mueller instead resurrected FARA from the near dead to go after people with the threat of jail time. The willful failure to register as an agent under FARA can result in five years in federal prison. Mueller also threatened to file FARA charges against former National Security Advisor Flynn to pressure him to cooperate—even though, again, Flynn had nothing to tell. Mueller would ultimately bring seven FARA cases, rivaling the total number brought by the DOJ in the prior fifty years. Nearly all of these were done in the context of plea deals, meaning Mueller did not have to test them in court.

Good-government types would laud Mueller for resurrecting a law against "shadowy" lobbying. But justice is never served by arbitrary or surprise shifts in the prosecutorial system. The most unjust law is one that is enforced only when it serves the purpose of catching the unwary. Mueller exploited the unsuspecting for his own ends. And his untoward tactics would end up boomeranging on the very Democrats who'd celebrated him. In an attempt to look more evenhanded, Mueller would at the very end outsource a FARA case against Gregory Craig, a prominent Democrat who'd served as White House counsel for Obama but who'd done Ukrainian lobbying work alongside Manafort.

Mueller razed another bedrock principle of our justice system in his pursuit of Michael Cohen, Trump's personal lawyer. In April 2018, the FBI raided Cohen's office, home, and hotel room, searching his files and riding roughshod over attorney-client privilege. That privilege has its roots in sixteenth-century English law, and was designed to encourage full communications between clients and lawyers, without fear that the government would intrude. There is a limit—what's called the crime-fraud exception—concerning communications that are used to further a crime.

But the Cohen case was messy, and his records didn't necessarily fall into clear crime-fraud exception. What's worse, the raiders were pushing this envelope in aid of an uncertain "crime." They were in part searching for evidence about a Cohen payment to adult film star Stormy Daniels, said to have had an affair with Trump. Prosecutors would go on to claim that Cohen, in paying this "hush money," had criminally broken federal campaign finance law by providing an undisclosed campaign contribution. This was an extraordinary stretch of campaign finance law. About 96 percent of all campaign finance violations are dealt with in civil suits. And prosecutors in the past had failed to advance the legal claim they were now pursuing against Cohen. The DOJ in 2012 lost in court a similar case against Democrat John Edwards for payments made by campaign donors to his mistress.

So yes, the crime-fraud exception has limits. But as former Attorney General Michael Mukasey asked in the *WSJ*, was it worth "testing" those limits, and undermining that principle, for a "campaign-finance" violation? The press would spend months dredging up legal experts to make the case that New York prosecutors and Mueller had done everything by the book—nothing to see here. But Mueller had sent the message that nothing is sacred—not even your conversations with your lawyer. If a special counsel wants it, he will get it. That has already had a chilling effect in law offices across the country.

Cohen and Gates ultimately succumbed to plea deals. Manafort fought his charges, but after a Virginia jury found him guilty on eight counts in 2018, he agreed to cooperate with Mueller's probe. It's important that we respect jury verdicts, and Manafort may never leave prison for the crimes of which he was duly convicted. At the same time, it's unlikely any of those men would have faced legal peril if not for their simple proximity to the man the haters truly wanted: Trump. How many Americans in the future will blanch from serving under or alongside controversial politicians, for fear they may be ensnared in a politically driven prosecution? Post-Mueller, that's a legitimate question.

The argument that Mueller was obliged to pursue any crimes he came upon is also undercut by his decision to ignore wrongdoers—when it suited him. The special counsel never brought a single prosecution for leaking, even though the leak of classified Flynn information remains, to this day, the only known "crime" of the time period Mueller was asked to investigate. Congressional Republicans would later send several criminal referrals to the Department of Justice against people it claimed had lied in the course of their investigation—including Steele. Mueller would never touch one of them.

New York prosecutors, working alongside Mueller, brought their dubious campaign finance charges against Cohen. Yet nobody in the Clinton orbit has faced prosecution for hiding from the public who ultimately paid for the dossier. Campaigns are supposed to list their "vendors," but the Clinton campaign and the DNC never listed Fusion GPS. The payment to Fusion was instead through a law firm cutout, Perkins Coie. *Somebody* was ignoring the clear language of campaign finance statutes.

Mueller revived FARA but largely used it only against those he wanted to put in a jam. Senator Chuck Grassley has suggested Fusion GPS was required to register under FARA both for its contribution to the lobby effort against a U.S. sanctions law (the Magnitsky Act) and for its work on the dossier. Fusion claims it had no such obligation. It is an untested question, though undoubtedly one Mueller would have brushed aside if he'd been treating Fusion as he treated Flynn or Manafort.

All of this meanwhile followed rival FBI investigations into presidential candidates, in which the bureau treated one side (Clinton) with kid gloves and the other (Trump) with an iron fist. In announcing Cohen's plea deal, Deputy U.S. Attorney Robert Khuzami waxed lyrical: "His day of reckoning serves as a reminder that we are a nation of laws, with one set of rules that applies equally to everyone."

The problem is that a significant portion of America no longer believes that.

* * *

A second category of Mueller prosecutions involved process crimes—individuals who were sentenced only because of actions they took while dealing with Mueller or federal officials. These included Papadopoulos, Alex Van der Zwann, and Flynn—all accused of making false statements to federal investigators.

The "false statements" charge has always been the last refuge of prosecutorial scoundrels. Comey used it on more than one occasion, to jail people he could not otherwise find guilty of a crime. And that's what is notable about Mueller's "lying" charges: They all came at the point at which it was clear to Mueller that he wasn't going to find Russian collusion. The "false statements" cases were his consolation prizes, his way of looking as if he had done "something."

And even many of these "lying" cases were flimsy. The Papadopoulos plea deal, for instance, shows a special counsel team straining to make the case against the former Trump aide. Papadopoulous's April conversation with Mifsud was supposed to be what inspired this entire FBI probe. But it took the Bureau nine months to formally interview Papadopoulos. The former aide sat willingly and would later testify that he thought he was there to assist the FBI. The FBI would instead turn around and charge him with lying about whether he was officially part of the Trump campaign when he had his conversation with Mifsud. The Mueller team would labor to explain how these "lies" had materially impeded their investigation, in particular their ability to fully question Mifsud when he was in the country in February 2017.

Papadopoulos to this day insists he did not intentionally lie to the FBI—that he simply misremembered dates—and that he was pressured into a plea deal. And the claim that confusion over those dates hurt the FBI's investigation is nonsensical. The FBI had known since at least July about the Mifsud communication. Mifsud in February talked to the FBI, and according to *The Hill* columnist John Solomon, then followed up by sending the FBI an e-mail. The FBI was in contact with Mifsud! It could have gone back to clarify issues. Papadopoulos was a minor figure in the Trump campaign, caught up in a sensationalized story that we now know was irrelevant. So why would prosecutors work so, so hard to get jail time? Because they needed a scalp.

More disturbing was Mueller's takedown of Flynn. The FBI had set up the Trump national security advisor—coaxing him into a meeting, dissuading him from using a lawyer, and then asking him about a conversation for which it already had a direct transcript. The interviewing agents also reported that they did not believe Flynn was lying to them. Mueller had all these documents; he should have been appalled.

Instead, he held out the "lying" charge, as well as a possible FARA prosecution, as he squeezed Flynn for information. And Mueller's team threatened a FARA charge against Flynn's son, Michael G. Flynn, who had lobbied with his father. The former lieutenant general had spent most of his adult life defending his country; he was not a rich man. As the investigation dragged on, Flynn's legal bills reached crippling heights, and he had to sell his home. He could have fought the charges, but with bankruptcy looming and with the FBI threatening a family member, he pleaded guilty to one count of lying. Flynn's defense team would give the court dozens of testimonials from military associates and from friends that attested to a lifetime of public service and a sterling character. Mueller's tactics against Flynn represented the worst sort of prosecutorial abuse, which is why the Department of Justice in May 2020 moved to drop the charges.

DOJ "false statements" charges are nothing new; Mueller didn't break ground here. What he did do is pursue highly questionable ones, as part of the biggest-profile investigation in decades. He reminded the entire nation that federal prosecutors are these days bullies, more interested in landing convictions than they are in pursuing their other duty of protecting the innocent. His tactics further undermined trust in the DOJ and the FBI.

* * *

The final group of Mueller charges: the only ones he was actually asked to pursue.

In February 2018, Mueller indicted a Russian troll farm (the Internet Research Agency), two shell companies, and thirteen Russian nationals on charges that ranged from conspiracy to defraud the United States to wire fraud to identity theft. The indicted are all foreign nationals and all live outside the United States, making it unlikely any will ever face trial. Mueller gets credit for exposing the methods Russians used to try to destabilize the U.S. political system, but this was also work that could have been done by the regular FBI.

When the DOJ announced the indictments, Rosenstein went out of his way to make clear they did not contain any allegation that "any American had any knowledge" of the Russian crimes. Mueller would nonetheless drag his probe out another year before presenting that conclusion in his report.

Throughout that year, Mueller would engage in a further dubious tactic: highly misleading and, at times, partisan court filings. The special counsel couldn't avoid presenting information as part of his plea deals and indictments. But it's one thing to present facts and quite another to present innuendo or hyped scenarios. Mueller with each filing fanned the Russia-collusion narrative— even in the absence of any proof of such a scandal.

His Papadopoulos plea deal stressed heavily that the young aide had engaged with "foreign nationals whom he understood to have close connections with senior Russian government officials." Such engagement is in no way a crime, and it is also totally irrelevant to the actual charge against Papadopoulos: lying to the FBI. The wording was designed to suggest the Russians might have been attempting to supply the Trump campaign with opposition research against Hillary—even though the document provides no proof this ever happened (because there never was any). A footnote in the plea deal similarly said that e-mails showed a Trump campaign official suggested "low level" staff should go to Russia. Mueller failed to include numerous other e-mails showing that the campaign was, in fact, directing people to turn down Russian invitations.

Mueller's December 2018 charging document against Cohen likewise goes out of its way to present every single interaction Cohen ever had with a Russian (no matter how meaningless), to puff up their importance, and to exclude important context. The document is at pains, for instance, to point out that Cohen e-mailed no less than Vladimir Putin's office twice in January 2016, in relation to talks to build a Trump Tower in Moscow. The document makes it sound as if there had been some secret communication line. But Paul Sperry, writing on *RealClearInvestigations,* pointed out that the document fails to note that Cohen did not have any direct contacts there and so was reduced to e-mailing a general mailbox. This fact, if anything, shows how *disconnected* the Trump team was from Russia. Yet, as Sperry noted, the press—true to form—seized on the Mueller misrepresentations. "Well into the 2016 campaign, one of the president's closest associates was in touch with the Kremlin on this project," exclaimed CNN's Wolf Blitzer. In case anyone missed it, he repeated: "Cohen was communicating directly with the Kremlin."

The press used every new court document to suggest that Mueller was closing the noose around Trump's neck. Mueller indulged this behavior, allowing a noxious cloud to continue spreading across the Trump administration, even though at the time of these filings he *knew* he had no evidence of collusion. His decision to do this can only be viewed in the worst light.

For the few media skeptics out there, each Mueller filing provided the opposite: more proof that the collusion narrative was growing ever more outlandish. Nowhere was this more clear than Mueller's final indictment against Roger Stone, which among other things accused him of lying to Congress about his interaction with WikiLeaks. Under the cloak of technical and serious legal terms, the indictment essentially describes a grasping Stone attempting to make himself look relevant to the Trump campaign. Stone tasks someone else with tracking down e-mails from WikiLeaks; he reaches out to a radio talk show host who had once interviewed WikiLeaks founder Julian Assange. He gets nowhere, and can't even get the White House to call him back. This is how you operate a global plot? The *WSJ* in an editorial in January 2019 described it as "Keystone Kops Collusion."

The more the press reached to produce "collusion," the more absurd its conspiracy theories grew. Consider that Trump Tower meeting between Trump Jr. and Veselnitskaya. Based on the information that emerged, we were essentially told to believe that collusion was being conducted via the daisy chain of Putin operating through a Russian oligarch who was operating through an international singer who was operating through his PR guy who was operating through a lawyer who was setting up meetings with Donald Trump Jr. about an unrelated subject. Go figure.

* * *

The media breathlessly anticipated the Stone indictment as the one that would finally lay collusion bare. When Mueller failed to produce the goods, a sense of panic set in among the press and Democrats. Schiff sat down with Ignatius at the *Washington Post* (purveyor of the crazy Logan Act theory) to lay out a *new* collusion theory.

Schiff had spent the past two years accusing men like Page and Manafort of treason. He'd promoted wild theories, including that

Trump had directed Cohen to lie to Congress (Mueller's team issued a rare statement denying this report) and that Trump Jr. had placed mysterious phone calls to his father right before his Trump Tower meeting (the Senate Intelligence Committee shot this down). In his interview with Ignatius, he didn't want to talk about any of that. Page who? Manafort who? He wanted to talk about his new theory, that the source of Trump collusion lay in Trump's financial dealings with Moscow, in particular something shady to do with Deutsche Bank. Intriguingly, some of us had read the Deutsche Bank conspiracy theories before. Fusion GPS's Simpson had spun them as part of his House testimony. The media nonetheless pivoted to these new Schiff claims, even as it held out hope that Mueller would still come through with something on the collusion front. After all, he still hadn't announced the end of his investigation.

Mueller might never have wrapped it up had it not been for Trump's appointment of William Barr. Barr was an inspired choice for attorney general. He'd done the job before, and had been respected on both sides of the political aisle. He was great in a crisis, particularly internal ones. In his first swing as AG, he'd overseen a CIA scandal and fallout from the Iran-Contra Affair. He was no-nonsense, with a reputation for searing intellect and strong principles. And he didn't need the job. At age sixty-eight, Barr had no interest in leveraging the post to new professional heights. He was genuinely taking the job out of a sense of duty. "I have a very good life, I love it—but I also want to help in this circumstance and I am not going to do anything I think is wrong, and I will not be bullied into doing anything I think is wrong, by anybody," declared Barr at his confirmation hearing.

Democrats didn't want any effective oversight at Justice, and many turned on Barr as soon as he was nominated. When they realized Republicans wouldn't be scared out of the nominee, they began pushing for Barr to recuse himself from the Russia investigation—on the grounds that as an outside citizen he'd written a memo on a narrow legal question of presidential obstruction. It was a frivolous complaint, and true to his word, Barr refused to be bullied into recusing. He was confirmed on a largely party line vote on Valentine's Day 2019.

It is no coincidence that Mueller finished only a few weeks later. The special counsel had gotten away with everything in the absence of effective DOJ oversight. John Dowd, who served as a Trump defense attorney and interacted with the special counsel team during its probe, told the *Washington Examiner*'s Byron York that Mueller had exhausted all of his witnesses and evidence by December 2017, and knew there was nothing to the Trump-Russia claims. Dowd separately blistered the special counsel for dragging the probe on for more than a year longer. "It's been a terrible waste of time," Dowd told ABC News in February 2019. "This is one of the greatest frauds this country's ever seen. I'm just shocked that Bob Mueller didn't call it that way and say, 'I'm being used.' I would've done that." Dowd added: "I'd have gone to Sessions and Rosenstein and said, 'Look.. This is nonsense. We are being used by a cabal in the FBI to get even.'"

But Barr was something else to reckon with, and Mueller hastily moved to close shop. He delivered his final 448-page report on March 22, 2019. Barr two days later released a summary of the report's principal conclusions, and less than a month after that released a largely unredacted version of the report to the public.

Volume I—on "collusion"—offered complete and total vindication for the Trump team, much to the haters' mortification. As with his indictments, the Mueller report sought to play up every tie, every meeting, every conversation between Trump folks and Russians. And yet the report had to acknowledge it could find no prosecutable evidence that the Trump campaign had coordinated in Russia's efforts to undermine the election.

It was an even greater vindication than that. A close read of the report showed that, if anything, the core Trump campaign

circle had been highly wary of Russian outreach and had repeatedly turned down offers of access. A close read also revealed just
how diligently and creatively the special counsel's legal minds had
worked to implicate someone, *anyone,* in Trump world on Russia-
related crimes. Mueller's people mulled bringing charges "for the
crime of conspiracy—either under statutes that have their own
conspiracy language" or "under the general conspiracy statute." It
debated going after them for the "defraud clause," which "criminalizes participating in an agreement to obstruct a lawful function
of the U.S. government." It considered the crime of acting as
an "agent of a foreign government." It pondered charging the
participants at the Trump Tower meeting with "a conspiracy to
violate the foreign contributions ban." It even credited Democrats' wild theory that Sessions had committed perjury at his
confirmation hearings and devoted a section to this in the report.
Yet after plowing through mountains of statutes, and subjecting
Team Trump to an investigative colonoscopy, Team Mueller utterly struck out.

The equally important takeaway from Volume I was (again)
what was *not* in it. A significant number of the allegations Mueller
had spent all that time investigating had come straight from a
dossier supplied by the rival political party. Mueller's failure to
establish the veracity of any of those claims was a searing indictment of the FBI and its decision to proceed with that document.
The nation had spent years engulfed in the dossier's conspiracy
theories, and Mueller had proved it all a hoax.

Yet his report said none of this. It mentions the dossier only in
passing, as part of bland descriptions of events. The Mueller team
almost deserved an award for the painstaking efforts it took to
write around the dossier, to pretend it played no role. One cost
of this naked effort to protect the FBI was that it meant Mueller
failed in a core mission. His job was to investigate Russian interference during the 2016 election. An obvious question is whether
the dossier was itself disinformation—whether Russians used

it to sow rumors and discord. Rosenstein's appointment order clearly allowed Mueller to investigate this question. Yet Mueller provided no evidence that he ever probed whether the collusion story was all backward—whether it had been the Clinton campaign and the DNC that had aided Russia in sowing discord. And he obviously never investigated the practices of the FBI itself.

Volume II—in which Mueller laid out his findings on presidential "obstruction"—was a different matter. Trump did himself no favors during the Mueller probe. His constant bashing of Comey and McCabe gave the disgraced FBI officials an opening to claim that Trump was responsible for diminished trust in intelligence community agencies (rather than their actions). His constant complaint that Mueller was on a "witch hunt" allowed critics to accuse him of attempting to obstruct the special counsel. More consequential, it inspired Mueller—out of pique or spite—to double down on his obstruction investigation. The special counsel got his revenge with Volume II.

Mueller spent 182 pages detailing every action Trump took from the firing of Comey to his tweets about Mueller—that might be construed as interfering in an investigation. Astoundingly, Mueller decided to make no "prosecutorial judgment" about all this. Instead, he said: "While this report does not conclude that the President committed a crime, it also does not exonerate him."

It was a stunning and cheap line, the special counsel's "Comey" moment. As responsible federal officials often remind their staff, neither the DOJ nor the FBI is in the business of smearing people. They are provided vast and intrusive tools, which they are supposed to use to conduct investigations. If at the end of those probes they do not find evidence persuasive enough to bring charges, that evidence is not made public. Comey was fired for giving a press conference in which he aired Clinton's dirty laundry, even as he refused to prosecute her. Everyone from the DOJ inspector general to former attorneys general agreed Comey's behavior was inexcusable.

Yet here was Mueller doing the *exact same thing*. It was never Mueller's job to "exonerate" Trump, as his cheap-shot line suggests. The DOJ does not exist to prove people are innocent. Mueller's job was to investigate Trump for crimes and decide if there was evidence enough to charge. Mueller conceded in his report that he lacked evidence to know Trump's motives in his actions. And as senior officials at DOJ would point out, Trump would have no reason to obstruct an investigation into *a crime his campaign didn't commit*. But instead of leaving it there, Mueller larded the report with unflattering details about Trump's private conversations with his staff, and with meandering legal theories about why all this might violate something or other. And note that Mueller only had all these ugly anecdotes because the Trump White House had complied with his every request, turning over millions of documents and making every witness available in person—save the president himself. The decision to release such a hit job was conduct unbecoming a government prosecutor.

Barr was meanwhile forced to step up and be the adult that Mueller had not been. In his initial summary of the conclusions, Barr explained that he was making the call on obstruction, and the DOJ would not pursue charges. Barr explained that he'd made this decision on the legal merits and completely aside from standing DOJ guidelines that hold a sitting president cannot be prosecuted. Barr explained that there simply was not sufficient evidence for obstruction charges.

The AG would later rightly question why Mueller had even pursued that half of the investigation, given he never intended to make a traditional prosecutorial judgment. At least some Republicans felt they knew why: Mueller was laying out a roadmap for Congress to pursue impeachment. And Mueller backed up that theory in late May, when he held a press conference. As the *WSJ* editorial page wrote in a piece titled "Mueller's Parting Shot": "The special counsel said the Russians he indicted for interfering in the 2016 election are innocent until proven guilty. About Mr.

Trump he said only that 'there was insufficient evidence to charge a broader conspiracy' between the Trump campaign and Russia." No one ever obstructed Mueller's probe, as evidenced by his fulsome report. He nonetheless went out of his way to weigh in for the Democrats who wanted to impeach Trump.

* * *

He did a bang-up job. While the haters were bitterly disappointed with his no-collusion findings, they latched on to the obstruction theme. Within weeks, Democrats had fired off volleys of subpoenas, demanding yet new documents and witness testimony from Trump's inner circle. The Trump White House—after having fully cooperated with Mueller—resisted. Democrats used that reticence to build on the "obstruction" meme—claiming that Trump, in refusing the legislative branch's sweeping demands, had provoked a "constitutional crisis."

Mueller also put his boss, AG Barr, in an untenable position. He dumped Volume II in Barr's lap, leaving the AG to clean up his "no-judgment" mess. Democrats instantly accused Barr of serving as Trump's lapdog. They also accused him of "hiding" things from them. Judiciary Committee Chairman Jerry Nadler sent Barr a subpoena demanding an entirely unredacted report, as well as all of Mueller's underlying investigatory material. Barr could not comply with the subpoena, since grand jury information is protected by federal law—as Nadler well knows. Nadler's committee nonetheless used the noncompliance as an excuse to vote Barr in contempt of Congress.

Meanwhile, on the eve of Barr's testimony to the Senate about the report, the Mueller team leaked a letter showing that the special counsel had not been thrilled with Barr's summary of his principal conclusions and had wanted the AG to quickly release parts of the report. Democrats hammered Barr, claiming this was proof that Barr had initially misrepresented the report's findings,

to better "protect" the president. Pelosi went so far as to accuse
the AG of lying to Congress. She similarly accused Barr of acting
as Trump's personal attorney rather than as "attorney general of
the United States."

These cowardly slurs fall at Mueller's feet. Barr offered
Mueller the opportunity to review his four-page summary before
he sent it to Congress. Mueller declined to do so, instead waiting
to complain until after the summary was made public. He meanwhile didn't call Barr to voice concerns; he memorialized his
unhappiness in an official letter. Prosecutors put things in letters
for only one reason—to later leak them and cause mischief. This
behavior, too, was reminiscent of Comey.

Mueller and his team proved as much a part of the Resistance
as the hooligans who marauded around Washington on Inauguration Day. They had the cover of fancy suits and sophisticated legal
language. But their aim was the same—to destroy the legitimacy
of a duly elected president and to provide Democrats ammunition
to remove him with impeachment proceedings.

But Mueller's Resistance mentality came with real costs. His
decision to use his post to undercut Trump—rather than simply
provide information—further divided an already bitter country.
He undermined long-standing powers of the presidency, in ways
that will plague future chief executives. And he chipped away
at long-standing legal principles—attorney-client privilege, equal
justice, uniform enforcement. In the process, he further destroyed trust in the very institutions—the Justice Department
and the FBI—that he had served so long.

CHAPTER 7

"DEEP STATE" REVOLT

If hell hath no fury like a woman scorned, Washington has no fury like a civil servant defied. Trump has no need to travel to a Resistance rally to meet his opponents; they work for him.

Trump and his circle have their own term for this particular group of resisters—the "deep state." I've used the phrase myself in speeches and in a column. The left likes to lecture people about the use of that term. They point out that it has traditionally been used to describe sinister cabals within foreign governments that rule by fiat, making the democratic process a facade. Fair enough, as no one would suggest that is what is happening in the United States.

Then again, most people understand Trump's meaning of the term. By "deep state," Trump is referring to any current or former federal employee who works to undermine him. I find that definition too broad, and it misses an important distinction. The Comeys and Brennans of the world were appointed to their jobs by politicians and are subject to a certain level of public scrutiny and political accountability.

"Deep-staters" to me are better defined as career civil servants who have growing amounts of power in our administrative state but who work in the shadows. These federal employees are tasked with processing government policy and decisions, and are supposed to do so with no judgment as to the political party in power. Many do. The federal government has plenty of honorable, talented, and hardworking individuals. But many others misuse their position. They have visceral political feelings and an unfortunate new willingness to act on them in the course of their duties.

The problem of an unaccountable federal bureaucracy is nothing new, and it hardly began with Trump. As government grows, so do the number of federal employees. And the more civil servants there are, the harder it is to keep track of shenanigans.

Many of these civil servants work for the government because they *believe* in big government; they already lean left. And they were turbocharged by an Obama administration that ruled by regulation and executive order, thereby handing to the bureaucracy decisions that are supposed to be made by an elected legislature. The career bureaucracy was put in charge of vast new programs—regulating energy, transportation, water, health care, taxes, finance. And as the Obama administration had no interest in policing them, they were left to run the show. This is the bureaucracy Trump inherited—big, bold, overweening.

Bureaucratic rebellions are also not new. One of the more famous takedowns happened to Anne Gorsuch—mother of Supreme Court justice Neil Gorsuch. Reagan appointed Anne Gorsuch in 1981 to run the EPA. The bureaucracy resented that she was an attorney and a reformer, rather than a card-carrying environmentalist. She cut the agency's budget and staff, hired people from industry in order get more diverse views, and pared back onerous regulations. EPA's career civil servants revolted and began leaking documents and planting stories with the press to undermine Gorsuch. Their machinations ultimately helped inspire a congressional investigation into the handling of the Superfund program. She didn't last even two years on the job.

But today's "deep state" is more dangerous. Our left-leaning civil bureaucracy is always hostile to Republican presidents, though mostly because they dislike conservative policies. Today's

federal bureaucracy is motivated by more than ideological differences; they despise Trump the man. An analysis by *The Hill*
newspaper in October 2016 that looked at employees at fourteen federal agencies concluded that 95 percent of their campaign donations had gone to Hillary Clinton. Imagine running
a company where 95 percent of your workforce is opposed to
your leadership.

Emboldened by modern federal employment rules that make
it all but impossible to fire bad actors, civil servants have proved
willing to take ever more outrageous actions to defy Trump—
some potentially illegal. Our modern society meanwhile gives
them more tools with which they can cause problems. They
use technology to keep in real-time connection with fellow bureaucratic resisters, anti-Trump groups, and the press, and they
use social media to transform their anti-Trump campaigns into
overnight scandals.

These deep-staters are in fact a big reason why the initial
warnings about Trump-as-dictator were overwrought. As the *WSJ*
editorial page wrote in the run-up to the 2016 election: "The
least convincing Never Trump argument is that he would ram-
page through government as an authoritarian. That ignores the
checks and balances in Washington that constrain GOP Presidents
in particular." Among these, we wrote, was "the permanent bureaucracy [that] would resist his political appointees, working
with the media to build public opposition."

The bureaucratic resistance has used their power to delay
and undermine Trump proposals, leak government information, team up with Trump opponents, spark an impeachment
furor, and gin up controversies that helped to run Trump cabinet heads out of Washington on a rail. The deep-staters like to
call themselves "whistleblowers," but that's a bastardization of an
honorable word. Whistleblowers expose government fraud or
corruption; the resisters are protesting the government policy
they are paid to implement. In doing so, they are delegitimizing

the very government they claim to serve and want to support. Government workers are a vital part of a civil society. Yet voters have become deeply suspicious of the federal bureaucracy and increasingly believe its members are hostile to democracy and the country's well-being. Yet more fallout from the Resistance.

* * *

Unfortunately for the country, government-employed resisters received a loud and ugly call to action within weeks of the new administration. Obama appointee Sally Yates became the acting attorney general upon Trump's inauguration and Loretta Lynch's departure. Yates was clearly gunning for the Trump administration, as she'd prove with her disingenuous Logan Act theories about National Security Advisor Michael Flynn. One week into his job, Trump signed his travel ban order. Almost immediately, Yates sent out a mind-bending memo to all Department of Justice staff, ordering lawyers not to defend any legal challenges to the order. Yates dramatically stated that it was her job to ensure "this institution's solemn obligation to always seek justice and stand for what is right." She went on to explain that she was not convinced the Trump order was "consistent with these responsibilities" or even "lawful." "For as long as I am Acting Attorney General, the Department of Justice will not present arguments in defense of the Executive Order," she decreed.

Trump took her at her word and fired her that same day. And it was outrageous that she forced him to do so. If Yates felt unable—legally or morally—to defend the executive order, she needed to resign. This is what every honorable prior cabinet secretary had done when faced with a similar situation. She had no business defying the chief executive, for whom she worked. The country elected Trump president, not Yates.

Yates's memo served as the first official act of the Resistance, and it did more than just set a terrible precedent for future of-

ficials. It served as a rallying cry for the Resistance within the
sweeping federal bureaucracy. Yates's belligerence was greeted
with fawning praise, as was exposed by e-mails obtained by Judicial Watch. "You are my new hero," wrote one United States
attorney. One DOJ colleague e-mailed: "Thank you AG Yates.
I've been in civil/appellate for 30 years and have never seen an
administration with such contempt for democratic values and the
rule of law. The President's order is an unconstitutional embarrassment and I applaud you for taking a principled stand against
defending it." And then there was Andrew Weissmann, the career
DOJ head of the Criminal Fraud Division, who went on to work
for Mueller. "I am so proud," Weissmann e-mailed her. "And in
awe. Thank you so much." Bureaucrats across the government
geared up: If Yates could use her post to defy the president, why
shouldn't they, too?

That rebel mentality helped feed the flood of leaks that accompanied the Trump presidency. While many of these undoubtedly
came from departed Obama political appointees, media stories
made clear that the leaks had also been corroborated by government employees working in the new administration. It's almost
impossible that the information was coming from newly installed
Trump political appointees; they hadn't been there long enough
to even know what was going on and had no interest in undercutting their new boss. Career civil servants were behind the
leaks. And those who leaked classified information committed
felonies—all in aid of undermining Trump.

Resistance employees also started using social media to "resist"
the administration. A National Park employee had already used
an official NPS Twitter account to troll Trump, passing along a
post that showed side-by-side pictures of the crowds at Trump's
inauguration versus Obama's. A former NPS employee would
a few days later hijack a government account to tweet about
climate change. Around the time of the Yates firing, someone
in the Defense Department set up a new Twitter handle called

@Rogue_DOD, on which was posted a damaging opinion piece about Trump and internal documents about climate change. A former employee at the Centers for Disease Control and Prevention set up @viralCDC, with the description: "The unofficial 'Resistance' page of the CDC." Its pinned tweet read: "If they choose to make facts controversial, the purveyors of facts must step into the controversy. #ScienceMarch #resist."

A January 31, 2017, *Washington Post* story reported those details, as well as that "180 federal employees have signed up for a workshop next weekend, where experts will offer advice on workers' rights and how they can express civil disobedience." It also reported that some "federal employees have set up social media accounts to anonymously leak word of [Trump administration] changes," and that others were in "regular consultation with recently departed Obama-era political appointees" about how to push back, and that yet others were planning to "slow" work if asked to focus on anything other than their policy "mission." It quoted an anonymous employee: "You're going to see the bureaucrats using time to their advantage . . . people here will resist and push back against orders they find unconscionable."

At the State Department, resisters organized a "cable" protesting Trump's travel ban, which worked its way through dozens of U.S. embassies and ultimately garnered at least 1,000 signatures. The cable was technically part of a "dissent channel" that Foggy Bottom maintains to allow officials to disagree with policy, and it is meant to be a confidential form of communication. The resisters nonetheless wasted no time in making the letter public, bragging about the numbers of signers and anonymously slamming Trump. The *WSJ* quoted an unnamed State Department official explaining the "overwhelming disgust and shock at this executive order. The general sense among career folks at State is that this is an affront to the values and interests we uphold every day on the world stage." Imagine if an employee of a private company were to engage in such sabotage of his employer? Then consider how much more inappropriate it is for a federal worker funded by taxpayers to undercut a chief executive. It was left to then–White House Press Secretary Sean Spicer to remind this career staff that they could either "get with the program or they can go." But like Yates, they lacked the integrity to do the right thing, and instead chose to abuse their posts for political gain.

A former Obama assistant secretary of state, Tom Malinowski, snarkily acknowledged to the *Post* that all this was an unprecedented, singular protest of Trump himself: "Is it unusual?... There's nothing unusual about the entire national security bureaucracy of the United States feeling like their commander in chief is a threat to U.S. national security. That happens all the time. It's totally usual. Nothing to worry about." This gives a sense of the depth of loathing of the Obama team to their successors, a view mirrored by huge swathes of the civil servant ranks.

Newspapers reported on agency staffers who continued to defiantly put out reports that contradicted official White House positions—especially on the issue of climate change. Some departments scrambled to rename and relabel cherished programs that conflicted with administration goals, to spare them any cuts.

* * *

In May 2017, I ran a column titled "Anatomy of a Deep State," which profiled Francesca Grifo, who within the EPA holds the title of "Scientific Integrity Official" (and no, that is not a joke). Obama set up the office in hopes of squelching any more debate over liberal science like climate change. Ms. Grifo had been a longtime activist at the far-left Union of Concerned Scientists, where she liked to complain that EPA scientists were "under siege" by Republican "political appointees" and "industry lobbyists" who had "manipulated" science. When she was hired in 2013 to run the EPA post, *Science* magazine explained that her job would be to lead an entire Scientific Integrity Committee, write an annual report documenting science "incidents" at the agency, and even "investigate" science problems—alongside no less than the agency's inspector general. And she was not a political appointee; her job came with "civil service protections." Meaning, she could not easily be fired.

Within five months of Trump's inauguration, Grifo reminded her EPA higher-ups of who was really in charge. In May, she sent out an invitation to a select group of about forty-five people to a June meeting in Washington. The invitation explained that they'd been asked to attend to develop "future plans for scientific integrity" at the EPA. Who was invited? Of the forty-five, only one invitee—the American Chemistry Council—was representative of the industries that the EPA regulates. A couple of academics also got invites. But the rest? Earthjustice. Public Citizen. The Natural Resources Defense Council. Center for Progressive Reform. Public Employees for Environmental Responsibility. Environmental Defense Fund. And a whopping three invites for Grifo's former employer—the Union of Concerned Scientists. The meeting represented a government employee using taxpayer funds to gather political activists to government grounds to plot out ways to undermine the Trump administration. Pretty cheeky, right? This has been par for the course in the Trump civil service ranks.

Holdovers from the Obama administration actively worked to cause mayhem and, when they were called out, dramatically resigned. A case study was Walter Shaub, whom Barack Obama appointed in 2013 to run the Office of Government Ethics. The OGE isn't a watchdog or an inspector general's office. It doesn't adjudicate complaints, investigate ethics violations, or prosecute. Rather, it was set up in 1978 to *help* the White House; its web page notes it is there to "advise" and to "assist" the executive branch in navigating complex ethical questions.

Trump came to office with more of those than most, and the OGE might have been an immensely valuable resource. Instead, within weeks of the election, Shaub was trolling the president-elect online, using the official OGE Twitter account to post tweets that mimicked Trump's style. "@realDonaldTrump OGE is delighted that you've decided to divest your businesses. Right decision!" "@realDonaldTrump Brilliant! Divestiture is good for you, very good for America!" When Trump finally released his plan for his assets, Shaub blasted it at a public event with press in attendance. It made clear Shaub had no intention of "helping" the White House navigate anything.

The pious political operator would go on to ride herd on the Trump team, releasing public letters detailing his gripes. Shaub at one point sent one of his complaining missives to hundreds of government ethics officials, every inspector general, and the chairmen and ranking members of numerous congressional com mittees. When Trump administration officials finally began to call him out on his outrageous behavior, he resigned in July in high dudgeon—though not before taking a grandstanding tour of every TV show that would have him. He, of course, immediately took a job with the liberal Campaign Legal Center, where he proceeded to more openly express his hatred of the man he was supposed to have assisted in office.

Bureaucrats also began filing official internal complaints, demanding to get to define their own policies and programs. In July 2017, an Interior Department employee named Joel Clement published an article in the *Washington Post* under the headline: "I'm a Scientist. I'm Blowing the Whistle on the Trump Administration." He began his piece: "I am not a member of the deep state," before going on to explain the many ways he was. He explained that he had just filed a complaint with the U.S. Office of Special Counsel—a federal body that both regulates and protects civil servants. Why? Clement had worked at Interior for seven years, in particular helping "endangered communities in Alaska prepare for and adapt to a changing climate." But now he, along with more than two dozen other senior career Interior employees, had been reassigned to a different job, working in the fossil fuel arena. Clement claimed this reassignment was in retaliation against him, "for speaking out publicly about the danger that climate change poses to Alaska Native communities," and called himself a "whistleblower." He also officially complained to the government that leaving his post empty would "exacerbate the already significant threat to the health and safety" of Alaska Natives.

Departments have broad authority to reassign top career employees like Clement. And Clement didn't get to decide what was a vital area of policy or not—that is left to a Congress that writes laws, and the elected and appointed officials of the executive branch that administers those laws. His complaint nonetheless inspired eight Senate Democrats to demand an Interior inspector general report. Notably, that 2018 report did not find evidence of Clement's charges of retaliation; as then–Deputy Interior Secretary David Bernhardt noted, the department's actions were entirely "lawful." Clement in the fall of 2017 would resign, with a much-publicized letter to Interior Secretary Ryan Zinke that made clear his complaint had always been about politics: "Secretary Zinke, your agenda profoundly undermines the [Department of Interior] mission and betrays the American people." Clement would go on to take a job—surprise—at the uber-left Union of Concerned Scientists.

In December, these acts of defiance led *The Atlantic* to declare 2017 the "Year of the Civil Servant." The article hailed the bureaucracy for toiling through "the president's chaotic first year in office," and continuing "the essential work of administering federal programs." It then congratulated those who had undercut or defied the administration's agenda: "They've also influenced the direction of government in 2017 in subtle, but crucial, ways: by containing some of the excesses of a new administration and by pushing the White House toward sounder policy outcomes." It saluted those who had fought against an administration that had made it "nearly impossible" for them to "do their jobs."

There is nothing impossible about showing up for work and implementing the policy agenda of those the voters elected to office. What's an impossible situation, for the future of the country, are huge swathes of a federal workforce that believe they get to call the shots. By the end of 2018, Resistance bureaucrats had grown so brazen that they didn't even blink about anonymously trashing superiors, and in the vilest language. A November 2018 story in the *Daily Beast* about the appointment of Matthew Whitaker as acting attorney general quoted a "trial attorney inside the [DOJ]" on his new boss: "He's a f—g tool."

* * *

Resistance deep-staters aren't alone in their anti-Trump work. They have a new, thriving, and growing outside network to help spread their leaks and tie up the internal works. Together, this triad of internal resisters, outside activists, and left-leaning press have pioneered a new form of the political takedown. It piles manufactured scandal upon manufactured scandal to create the pressure necessary to drive Trump cabinet heads out of their jobs.

The left loves to disparage "dark money" and conservative nonprofits. They bitterly complain about Supreme Court decisions such as Citizens United that allow for free speech and a thriving nonprofit community. They spent years accusing watchdog organizations like Judicial Watch of hounding the Obama administration. But if imitation is the sincerest form of flattery, Judicial Watch has a lot of admirers in the Trump era.

Within months of Trump's inauguration, progressive nonprofits started popping up all over Washington—set up by powerful liberal political players (many of them Obama and Clinton alumni), funded by sources unknown, and united in burying the Trump administration under a mountain of scandal. They instantly teamed with the internal Resistance.

These are groups like Democracy Forward, which launched in 2017 with a mission to litigate the Trump administration into the dust. The board at launch included Marc Elias, the Perkins Coie lawyer behind the infamous Steele dossier, and John Podesta, chairman of Hillary Clinton's 2016 campaign. It has a big operation as these things go, with a staff composed largely of Obama administration lawyers and advisers. It instantly started filing lawsuits against the administration on everything from immigration policy to health care rules.

American Oversight, also created in 2017, billed itself as "the top Freedom of Information Act ligitator investigating the Trump administration." Its chief counsel had served eight years in the Obama Justice Department. Restore Public Trust, which launched in 2018, explained its mission was to "expose corruption and malfeasance at the highest levels of government." Its executive director, Caroline Ciccone, was a longtime DNC and Obama campaign surrogate, and her board was stacked with former Obama and Clinton people. A *Daily Beast* headline on its launch day spelled out the mission: "New Progressive Oversight Group Wants to Make Trump's Cabinet Miserable."

Plenty of longtime Washington progressive groups had already been doing just that: Public Citizen, the Center for Public Integrity, Citizens for Responsibility and Ethics in Washington, the Campaign Legal Center, the Sierra Club, the NRDC. Working alongside them were liberal think tanks like the Center for American Progress, and leftist press "watchdogs" such as Media Matters. This network of pressure groups allied with rebellious federal bureaucrats and started claiming Trump scalps.

Trump named Scott Pruitt to lead the EPA in December 2016, and many conservatives were thrilled by the appointment. Pruitt had been the highly successful attorney general of Oklahoma and a fierce critic of the Obama EPA's extralegal actions. Pruitt vowed to take the EPA back to basics. "Agencies exist to administer the law. Congress passes statutes, and those statutes are very clear on the job the EPA has to do. We're going to do that job," Pruitt told me in an interview the *WSJ* ran in February 2017.

Democrats and EPA bureaucrats despised Pruitt for that very

mentality, and EPA staff was openly hostile to his leadership—more so than workers at any other agency. Newspapers reported how EPA resisters were calling their senators, urging them to vote against Pruitt's confirmation. They openly provided quotes disparaging the nominee. The union representing EPA employees sent e-mails and Facebook and Twitter messages "urging members to reject him," detailed the *New York Times*. Chicago EPA employees engaged in a demonstration against the nomination, holding signs that read: "We Want Clean Air and Clean Water!" (Who doesn't?) Jeffrey Holmstead, a senior EPA official back in the George W. Bush administration, acknowledged to the *NYT* that "I don't remember, in my time, anything like this. But I think that anyone Trump nominated would be targeted."

And that was Pruitt's mistake—not taking that threat seriously. Even in the face of explicit warnings. In January 2017, the far-left environmental group NRDC ran a piece on its website titled "Scott Pruitt: You've Been Warned." It went on to read: "Pruitt may have cleared the ethics bar, but he shouldn't get too cocky. The last time a fervently anti-regulation, pro-industry ideologue took over the reins at the EPA, it ended very badly—for the EPA director, I mean." The author was referencing Anne Gorsuch, whom the bureaucracy had taken out in two years.

Pruitt should have handcuffed himself to an ethics lawyer the minute he walked into his office. Especially because he *was* effective—one of Trump's most productive reformers. As the *WSJ* editorial board wrote: He "started to roll back the Obama administration's Clean Power Plan that attempted to re-engineer the economy with little effect on climate change. He clamped down on the 'sue and settle' racket that allows environmental groups to impose policy through consent decrees. He moved to redefine the Waters of the United States rule, that let EPA regulate ponds and potholes. Mr. Pruitt also sought to require more honest cost-benefit analysis." These successes further infuriated bureaucrats in an agency that had become the tip of the progressive, green spear.

Pruitt unfortunately also provided the left all the fodder it needed to turn a million little molehills into a mountain. Internal resisters began leaking documents to outside activists and the press; each little dot and jot became a "scandal." They targeted his air travel, his requests to his staff, his meetings with members of industry. They went after his spending, which included taxpayer dollars for customized fountain pens and for a soundproof phone booth (particularly dumb moves on Pruitt's part). They engaged in a protracted drama over a small condo in D.C. that Pruitt had briefly rented from casual friends. The haters pounced on the fact that the condo was co-owned by a woman whose husband owned a lobby firm representing energy industry players. The husband had no share in the condo and he had no lobby contact with the EPA in 2017 or 2018. The EPA's principal deputy general counsel released a memo explaining that EPA career ethics officials had reviewed the lease and found that Pruitt paid a "reasonable market value."

But the endless internal leaks and hits created a D.C. meme that Pruitt was irredeemably "corrupt." Even some conservatives began labeling Pruitt as part of the "swamp." The campaign had two goals—to drive Pruitt out and to send a message to other cabinet members: We run things here, and if you attempt to change the system, we will destroy you. It was without doubt the most brazen and unprofessional bureaucratic rebellion in the history of U.S. politics. But it worked. Hamstrung by a barrage of ethics complaints, Pruitt resigned in July 2018.

Emboldened, the bureaucratic-activist complex seamlessly retrained its fire on another hated secretary: Interior's Ryan Zinke. The former Montana congressman had been similarly aggressive about reforming his sprawling department. He in particular had voiced his intention to once again use public lands "for the benefit and enjoyment of the people." The line, which comes from the Yellowstone National Park Protection Act of 1872, is the true definition of "conservation" and was once the guiding mentality of

Interior Department leadership. But many Interior bureaucrats are today captive to a green mentality that wants to put public lands off-limits to any use—energy extraction, snowmachining, fishing, even hiking.

Zinke also put forward exciting new plans to devolve more authority out to employees in the field, and maybe even relocate some of Interior's agencies to the West—closer to the lands they oversee. These innovative proposals were an opportunity for Interior's workforce. Instead, the D.C. mandarins worried about job security. And green bureaucrats and activists reviled Zinke's conservation approach.

Zinke never gave the haters as much ammunition as Pruitt did. Resisters nonetheless engineered at least fifteen investigations into everything from a Montana real estate deal, to Zinke's security detail, to whether (no joke) his wife could ride with him in government vehicles. Zinke submitted his resignation letter in December 2018. The haters also successfully smeared Ronny Jackson, Trump's nominee to become secretary of veterans affairs. Jackson, a rear admiral, had served as a respected White House physician for three administrations. Upon his nomination, unnamed White House medical staff—part of that deep-state Resistance—accused Jackson of creating a hostile work environment and of excessive drinking. None of this was ever proven, but the "scandal" was such that Jackson withdrew himself from consideration—another personal casualty of the Resistance smear campaign.

Could the Pruitts of the administration have been far more careful in their actions and done a lot more to hew to ethics regimes? Absolutely. And they should have; they were working for a president who had promised to drain the swamp. The takedowns at least served as a wake-up call to other Trump officials, too many of whom came into D.C. unprepared for the coming onslaught. Yet at the same time the bureaucrats and activists created a dangerous new standard in Washington. Many talented and qualified—and highly ethical—people have since passed on opportunities to work in the Trump administration. They have no desire to have their personal lives ransacked and their reputations smeared, or to open themselves up to litigation—which is now a risk even for people who do nothing wrong.

The Resistance might call this a victory. But don't we want highly qualified people serving their country? And if the Resistance truly does think Trump is a danger, don't they want capable people around him? This model—which the Resistance has turned into the "new norm" in Washington—will deter many other accomplished people from serving in government in future. That will be a loss to both Democratic and Republican administrations, and to the country.

* * *

Nearly every mainstream news story about Trump and the federal workforce lays the dysfunction on the president. Trump has crippled government morale. Trump is causing a federal brain drain. A March 2018 *Politico* story even blamed Trump for provoking "anxiety," "depression," and "heavier drinking" among the federal bureaucracy.

Responsibility for said misery and exits rests with the bureaucracy itself. Every American has the right to a political view and a vote. But federal employees don't have the right to carry those views into their work environment and act upon them. Millions of civil servants prior to 2016 managed to faithfully discharge their duties under both Republican and Democratic presidents. Those who revolted against Trump have undermined the professionalism of their colleagues, sowed greater distrust in the civil servant class, and leaked damaging confidential and classified information. Mostly, they have discouraged Americans in the future from serving their government—whether at the appointed or the staff level. All are further consequences of the over-the-top reaction to the 45th president.

CHAPTER 8

JUDICIAL UNRESTRAINT

It was July 2016. Both Donald Trump and Hillary Clinton were gearing up for their nomination conventions. Republicans were still going rounds over whether Trump was a good face for the party, whether he'd govern the way he'd campaigned, and whether he even had a shot at beating Clinton. Into this discussion wandered the least likely, and least appropriate, of voices: Supreme Court Justice Ruth Bader Ginsburg.

High court justices don't often give interviews. And they never criticize political candidates. Yet Ginsburg in July sat down with the *New York Times* to unleash on Trump. "I can't imagine what this place would be—I can't imagine what the country would be—with Donald Trump as our president," she said. "For the country, it could be four years. For the Court, it could be—I don't even want to contemplate that." She suggested maybe now was the time to "move to New Zealand."

Ginsburg's comments were met with shocked disapproval from court watchers and legal scholars. George Washington University law professor Jonathan Turley pointed out that her comments were "thoughtless," but more importantly "they were facially unethical. Canon 5 of the judicial code says that judges cannot make statements of this kind in opposition to political candidates." Yet rather than apologize to her fellow members of the judiciary,

Ginsburg doubled down. Only a few days later she sat down with CNN and complained: "He has no consistency about him. He says whatever comes into his head at the moment. He really has an ego." She also called him a "faker."

Trump's election brought with it one particularly dramatic warning: Resisters insisted the rule of law would be trampled. The haters were right; the rule of law has been stomped. But it has been done by the very federal judiciary pledged to faithfully discharge the laws and Constitution of the United States.

The Resistance was overwhelmingly bitter over what a Trump presidency meant for the courts. A Clinton victory would have finally delivered them a liberal Supreme Court and a progressive jurisprudence that ended gun rights and political free speech. Their disappointment was palpable. What nobody might have imagined is that this profound discontent was fully shared by many members of the federal judiciary, or that some would act on it.

No one was surprised when Trump's critics quickly turned to the courts to oppose his actions. If anything, this was reassuringly normal. It is routine for the party out of power to mobilize its state attorneys general and activist groups to test the legality of a president's policies. Republicans filed piles of lawsuits against the Obama administration and racked up an impressive record of staying or overturning Obama's extralegal moves. Opposing parties can, of course, be overly litigious—challenging every little thing. But the courts exist to settle legal disputes.

What did surprise court watchers was the eagerness with which members of the federal judiciary accepted even crazy challenges and abandoned normal judicial practice in order to strike down Trump policy. The "normal judicial practice" point is key. We've always had splits in judicial *ideology*. Yet despite their vastly different readings of the law, federal judges are nonetheless expected to adhere to basic principles that are designed to maintain the integrity of the judiciary as a whole. Judges, for instance, are meant to ensure that those who come before the court have legitimate "standing" to bring a suit, to deter frivolous cases. They are discouraged from issuing nationwide injunctions, since those orders stifle legal debate. They are supposed to decide cases on the basis of statutes wherever possible and avoid immediately jumping to sweeping constitutional conclusions.

What distinguishes Resistance judges is their new willingness to throw over these norms, and the rule of law, in order to slap down Trump's policies. "It's one thing to have different approaches to constitutional or statutory interpretation," constitutional expert and Baker Hostetler partner David Rivkin tells me. "But if you are going to pretend to be a federal judge you have to start with a doctrine. If you instead start from the position 'how do I screw Donald J. Trump,' you aren't a real judge."

The Resistance judges have undermined both the law and the Constitution. They have also undermined the reputation of the courts, at a time when the public is already losing faith in core institutions like Congress and law enforcement. And they set new and potentially dangerous precedents that will outlast any Trump presidency. The country has traditionally looked to the courts to provide a less-partisan, more cool-headed judgment of disputes. The Resistance judges damaged that public belief.

* * *

Trump isn't shy about attacking the courts and judges, and that isn't actually so shocking. Judges are no strangers to criticism, and the public and officials have as much right to call out that branch as any other. Obama publicly complained about court decisions, and in 2010 he used a State of the Union Address to scorch the conservative majority of the Supreme Court for its Citizens United decision—with several of the justices sitting right in front of him. Making it worse, Obama accused the Supreme Court of allowing "foreign" corporate contributions in U.S. political campaigns—

which was patently false. (Lucky for Obama, his untruth was not greeted with rounds of press stories about his "lies.") Trump has occasionally taken shots at the Court's legitimacy—which is a bigger problem. Criticizing opinions is one thing; suggesting a court is rigged is another. At the same time, the White House has never come close to defying judicial authority.

More shocking has been judiciary members' willingness to take personal shots at the *president*—which is virtually unprecedented. Judges have ideologies, but they always take great care not to express partisan views. Ginsburg's comments on Trump were utterly inappropriate and did far more damage to the Court's reputation than anything Trump has said. How can Americans trust the Supreme Court to fairly judge a president's policies in light of comments like that?

Former Supreme Court Justice John Paul Stevens did further damage—and violated more norms—when he launched himself in 2018 into the partisan fight over Trump high court nominee Brett Kavanaugh. Stevens in a talk said he'd come to the conclusion that Kavanaugh didn't have the "qualifications" for the high court. He didn't doubt his "intellectual ability," but said Kavanaugh's decision to defend himself during his show trial hearing over sexual assault allegations demonstrated "political bias." It has always been the tradition of former justices to remain quiet during confirmation battles, but there was Stevens sounding like a mouthpiece for Democrats.

* * *

The judiciary's actions spoke even louder than these words. Nothing highlighted the lawless impulses of Resistance judges better than the first legal fight of the Trump administration: the travel ban. Trump signed his initial executive order on January 27, 2016, restricting travel into the United States from seven countries with terrorist ties. Trump opponents knew this was coming, and they were ready. Between January 28 and January 31 (the three days following the order), dozens of cases were filed in federal court. This flood of litigation was what inspired then–Acting Attorney General Sally Yates to issue her showboat memo ordering DOJ staff not to defend the executive order in court. Bye, bye, Sally.

Washington State was the first to file, and that case subsequently got the most attention. The speed with which the state's attorney general got his paperwork in showed the Resistance had been planning this a long time—and intended to sue no matter what the content of the executive order. The suit landed with a Seattle federal judge, James Robart. By February 3, Robart had ordered all parties to his courtroom, where he allowed oral argument for a mere hour. The judge complained about the "litany of harms" the ban was putting on Washington State and declared that for any order to be constitutional, it needed to be "based in fact, as opposed to fiction."

Robart that very same day then issued a national, and indefinite, halt to the travel order. It came in the form of a nonspecific written opinion, in which he failed to explain what exactly the travel order violated. He did not mention any statutes and did not spell out what part of the Constitution had been offended. The due process clause? The establishment clause? The equal protection clause?

Four days later, a three-judge panel on the Ninth Circuit heard the appeal. A mere two days later it upheld Robart, claiming the ban violated several parts of the Constitution. The Ninth Circuit was so eager to gets its hands on this case that it tried to sideline Robart— leading to confusion over who was actually handling the suit.

All these proceedings were moot in any event, since on March 6, the White House issued a replacement order, which applied to five majority-Muslim countries but also to North Korea and Venezuela. Hawaii sued to stop the new version two days later, and within a week a federal judge in Hawaii—Derrick Watson—

had issued another nationwide halt. The Ninth Circuit in June upheld his block. The Fourth Circuit Court of Appeals also got in on the act, and in May itself upheld a nationwide block on the ban. That appeals court completely ignored the statutes in question, in which Congress provided presidents significant executive authority over immigration policy. It instead jumped straight to a claim that Trump had ravaged the Constitution, excoriating the ban as one that "drips with religious intolerance." In finding this, it relied on things Trump had said on the campaign trail rather than the actual text of the order or Justice Department court filings. A third version of the ban came out in September. Opponents promptly sued and stopped it yet again.

It took the Supreme Court to put an end to the silliness; in early December, *seven* of its nine justices voted to allow the ban to take effect, pending the ongoing legal challenges. And in June 2018, the Supreme Court upheld the third version of the ban, on the grounds that Trump had clear and broad authority under the Immigration and Nationality Act to suspend the entrance of noncitizens to the country. Chief Justice John Roberts cited the clear text of the law, which allows for presidents to "suspend the entry of all aliens or any class of aliens" as they see fit. Roberts wrote that the provision "exudes deference to the president in every clause." The opinion also noted that as the order said nothing about religion, it presented no constitutional concerns.

The high court's ruling was obvious to anyone who had read the law and who knows that a president's authority is at its strongest when he acts with congressional consent. Which only highlighted all the more the prior year of judicial hysteria and claims of constitutional abuse.

* * *

The travel ban drama was a great case study in just how willing the judicial Resistance was to break norms in aid of thwarting

Trump. The problem wasn't that the courts had come up with flawed opinions. The problem was that they'd ignored all the usual safeguards that are meant to *protect* against frivolous lawsuits and flawed opinions. And it wasn't just one or two judges indulging in occasional reckless behavior. Dozens of judges and significant numbers of appeals courts began routinely trashing basic judicial norms. The practice has become so overt that the Supreme Court has on occasion felt compelled to chide the lower courts for ignoring first principles.

Take the bedrock doctrine of "standing"—the constitutional requirement that a plaintiff must show actual harm to be allowed to bring a lawsuit. Standing is crucial for deterring political lawsuits; we don't want courts becoming a venue for settling partisan disputes. Yet Resistance judges are so eager to allow cases against Trump and his administration that they are granting "standing" to anything with a heartbeat. A huge number of the plaintiffs who filed suit against the Trump travel ban had only the barest claim that the policy had harmed them—yet judges allowed the suits to proceed.

A great example came in March 2018, when U.S. District Judge Peter Messitte—a Clinton appointee—ruled that District of Columbia Attorney General Karl Racine and Maryland Attorney General Brian Frosh had legal standing to sue Trump over the business dealings of his Washington, D.C., hotel. The lawsuit claims Trump has violated the Constitution's "emoluments clause"—an obscure provision that bans public officials from accepting "any present" from "any King, Prince or foreign State" without "the Consent of the Congress." The Founders included the clause out of an eighteenth-century concern that U.S. ambassadors might be corrupted by fancy presents from European rulers. The clause has barely been talked about since.

The critics argue that the clause restricts Trump from benefiting in a way from money connected to a foreign state. They insist that any time a foreigner rents, say, a ballroom in a Trump hotel, the president is breaking the clause. Put aside that nobody has ever applied this to prior presidents—many of whom operated businesses while in office, which likely had foreign clients. Put aside that the money that goes to Trump's Washington hotel is not a "gift"—but rather payment for services rendered. And put aside that the Justice Department has said the emoluments clause does not apply to private business—only to benefits received in a public capacity.

The bigger issue are the words "without the consent of the Congress." To the extent courts had ever considered the emoluments clause over the past 200 years, it was understood that only Congress could enforce the provision. That's why a federal judge in 2017 dismissed a separate lawsuit brought by a liberal watchdog against Trump over the emoluments clause, writing: "Congress is the appropriate body to determine whether, and to what extent, Defendant's conduct unlawfully infringes on that power." Yet Judge Messitte took the unprecedented step of granting standing to two Democratic attorneys general, with no connection to Congress. An appeals court dismissed the suit in July 2019.

Or take the principle of constitutional avoidance—a doctrine drilled into law school grads. That doctrine emphasizes that federal courts should always seek to resolve a suit on the basis of a statute or regulation, and only turn to the Constitution as a last resort. The U.S. Supreme Court has routinely directed the lower courts to proceed in this manner. The high court understands that shouting "constitutional violation" is too easy a way to proceed on a lawsuit, since the Constitution is broad. Its directive is a recognition that often Congress will with specific language grant a president broad powers in a certain policy area. That grant makes it harder to claim that a president has violated the Constitution as he goes about his duties. The high court has explained that constitutional avoidance is necessary to ensure courts accord a "just respect" to both the legislative and the executive branches.

The travel ban mess illustrated perfectly what goes wrong

when courts ignore this. District court judges and appeals courts instantly ran to the Constitution, claiming Trump had violated everything from due process to the First Amendment. It took the Supreme Court to point out that Congress had granted the president sweeping powers with its Immigration and Nationality Act—which made the constitutional issues in that issue moot.

The Supreme Court has meanwhile had to rebuke Resistance judges that have taken to ruling on what Trump says, rather than what Trump does. When the Fourth Circuit Court in May 2017 upheld the block on Trump's travel ban, it said it was likely unconstitutional because it was driven by anti-Muslim sentiment. In backing up this opinion, the court cites "then-candidate Trump's numerous campaign statements expressing animus towards the Islamic faith." The Fourth Circuit utterly disregarded the stated policy arguments for the ban.

In the Supreme Court's own ruling on the final travel ban, Chief Justice Roberts smacked down this extralegal approach. "The issue before us is not whether to denounce the statements. It is instead the significance of those statements in reviewing a presidential directive, *neutral on its face*, addressing a matter within the core of executive responsibility," wrote Roberts (italics added). "In doing so, we must consider not only the statements of a particular president, but also the authority of the presidency itself."

Roberts went on to point out that the consequence of holding a president to anything he might have ever said (rather than what he did) would be to bar him from fulfilling his basic duties.

The high court majority also took a shot at lower courts' decision to drag in an infamous if completely unrelated case: Korematsu. That's the Supreme Court's 1944 decision upholding FDR's roundup and internment of people of Japanese descent. Resistance judges claimed Trump had done the same here—using a vague security threat to justify excluding people from U.S. society. The majority labeled this sheer baloney, stating that "Korematsu has nothing to do with this case," since that suit had called for the internment of American citizens "solely and explicitly on the basis of race." Trump's order bore no relation.

Perhaps the worst abuse has been the flurry of nationwide injunctions. The federal government has ninety-four district courts, which are the first stop for any federal lawsuit. The opinions from these district court judges can be appealed up to their respective circuit court (thirteen in all). And circuit court decisions can be appealed to the Supreme Court. It's long been understood that when a court issues a ruling, it applies only to the people who appear before it or to the area that the court covers. There's a constitutional issue at stake here. The Constitution says that a plaintiff must have standing in order to sue. Yet by definition, national injunctions impose law on millions of people who have no such standing.

The United States is a big place with a lot of judges, and the system is meanwhile specifically designed to encourage a bit of conflict. A district court judge in, say, Alaska is only required to follow the decisions of the Ninth Circuit. Each of the thirteen circuits is allowed to go their own way. Circuits routinely come up with conflicting opinions, a cue for the Supreme Court to step in to settle an issue. By the time the high court does, the question has often been debated and informed by the legal views of dozens of U.S. judges. A national injunction squelches this legal debate; it immediately imposes the view of one judge on the entire country. It is, in fact, an astonishing power grab, which is why such orders are usually shunned.

National injunctions also encourage what's known as "forum shopping." Instead of going through the usual system, litigants go straight to a judge or circuit where they figure they have the best shot of getting an immediate national order. It's no accident that so many of the lawsuits against the Trump travel ban were filed on the West Coast. It's part of the Ninth Circuit, which has proven itself notoriously willing over the years to push the boundaries of acceptable legal practice.

Nicholas Bagley, a law professor at the University of Michigan, also points out the sheer harm of stopping a national government program or policy in its tracks: "What I struggle with is why anyone would support handing to judges the authority to put a halt to important government programs just because they happen to get their knickers in a twist about a particular case," he told *The Hill* newspaper in 2019. Bagley was underlining just how out of keeping these injunctions are with the traditional court view that the office of the presidency is afforded great deference at least at the outset of a policy or executive order.

Obama sparked more than a few national injunctions, but the court use of these corrosive orders has absolutely skyrocketed under Trump. Litigants pile into district courthouses shouting "executive power abuse," and judges are only too willing to believe the hype and move instantly to shut down facially valid executive orders and policies. As of May 2018, the Trump administration had been the subject of no fewer than thirty-five national injunctions—more than any other administration combined going back to the 1960s. Changes to Obama's Dreamer program? National injunction. Ban on transgender service members? National injunction. Restrictions on asylum applications? National injunction.

Resistance judges in the Ninth Circuit have been so free-wheeling with nationwide injunctions against Trump policies that its appeals court stepped in to warn them against the abuse. "District judges must require a showing of nationwide impact or sufficient similarity to the plaintiff states to foreclose litigation in other districts, from Alaska to Puerto Rico to Maine to Guam," wrote Judge J. Clifford Wallace in December 2018. Wallace was speaking on behalf of a three-judge panel on the Ninth Circuit that was reviewing a nationwide ban against Trump rules governing contraceptive coverage under Obamacare.

Justice Clarence Thomas was so appalled by the growing use of these orders that he filed a concurring opinion to the Supreme

Court's travel ban decision. He blasted their use and sent a warning to judges. He's worth quoting at length, to provide a sense of just how off the rails the Resistance judges have gone:

> Injunctions that prohibit the Executive Branch from applying a law or policy against anyone . . . have become increasingly common. District courts, including the one here, have begun imposing universal injunctions without considering their authority to grant such sweeping relief. These injunctions are beginning to take a toll on the federal court system—preventing legal questions from percolating through the federal courts, encouraging forum shopping, and making every case a national emergency for the courts and for the Executive Branch.
>
> I am skeptical that district courts have the authority to enter universal injunctions. These injunctions did not emerge until a century and a half after the founding. And they appear to be inconsistent with longstanding limits on equitable relief and the power of Article III courts. If their popularity continues, this Court must address their legality.

* * *

One of the more astute observers of the judicial Resistance has been Josh Blackman, a professor of law at the South Texas College of Law and a scholar for Cato. Blackman has written prolifically on presidential legal questions. And he is an interesting case, in that he isn't a fan of a lot of Trump policy, but he does care deeply about the rule of law. As he wrote at one point: "In many respects, my work on [the travel ban] cases is a mirror image to my previous work on the constitutionality [of] President Obama's [immigration] policies [which granted some undocumented immigrants temporary status]. While I supported [those] as a matter of policy, I concluded they were unlawful. In contrast, while I oppose the travel bans as a matter of policy, I concluded they were lawful."

Blackman was one of the first people to call out the "legal resistance," and he's been particularly scathing about the tactics and the damage it has done to the judiciary. In a *National Review* article in October 2017, he addressed the travel ban maneuvers, pointing out the degree to which the Resistance had turned its strategy into a new legal art form:

> This judicial blitz was a dry run of the legal resistance's game plan. It would be repeated again and again with respect to the second iteration of the travel ban, sanctuary-city policies, and efforts to unwind the Obama administration's regulatory agenda. First, President Trump takes an executive action. Second, litigants file suit in multiple friendly forums. Third, the court disregards prudential barriers that restrict suits against the executive—a role exactly opposite to the one that the judiciary usually plays. Fourth, looking beyond the four corners of the policy, the court throws out the policy by psychoanalyzing the commander-in-chief based on his tweets, cable-news interviews, and even campaign statements. Finally, without affording the president the traditional deference his office is due, the court issues a nationwide injunction, stretching far beyond the judges' jurisdiction.

This "game plan" has been repeated ad nauseum. In June 2012, Obama issued a presidential memorandum on what is technically called the Deferred Action for Childhood Arrivals. Colloquially, we call it the Dreamers program. It made illegal immigrants who had been brought to the United States as children eligible to avoid deportation and acquire work permits.

I personally am an enormous fan of awarding legal status for Dreamers; they are here through no consequence of their own, have largely grown up in this country, and are for the most part productive contributors to our society. That being said, Obama's order was undeniably unlawful. Prior to issuing the order, he had repeatedly said he lacked the authority to do so—then did it anyway. He ordered the immigration services to ignore the law. He claimed this was just "prosecutorial discretion," but such power is usually a judgment call over individual cases—not applied to a sweeping class of hundreds of thousands of individuals. And several courts found the policy unconstitutional.

The Trump administration on September 5, 2017, announced it would repeal Obama's order—and what followed was the "game plan" to a tee. A flood of lawsuits hit the system within a week of the announcement—most of them in "friendly" jurisdictions. Trump had issued an executive order, just as Obama had issued an executive order. The Resisters claimed Trump's order was arbitrary and capricious—completely ignoring the administration's compelling arguments that DACA was unconstitutional. The courts owed as much deference to Trump as they did to his predecessor. Instead, they rushed to shut the new president down. In January 2018, San Francisco District Court Judge William Alsup issued a nationwide halt to Trump's policy and ordered the federal government to continue accepting renewal applications for the program. In his order, Alsup cited presidential comments and tweets to claim that Trump had an animus against Dreamers, and that he had taken this step only in order to have a "bargaining chip to demand funding for a border wall." Blackman noted in a subsequent piece about the ruling that "these talking points could have been plagiarized from the MSNBC chyron."

* * *

Judges have repeatedly indulged in similar behavior in court cases involving everything from sanctuary cities to the military's transgender ban. The damage to the judiciary has been profound and will be lasting.

Once a court plows new and extralegal ground, they set a precedent. Other courts feel free to take the same steps, or even expand on those excesses. Absent direct Supreme Court orders to cease and desist, we can assume Resistance judges will continue to ignore rules on standing or constitutional avoidance or national injunctions. Even some liberals are now coming to worry about this violation of judicial norms, as conservative judges feel more emboldened to adopt the same tactics. Several district judges are under pressure, for instance, to issue nationwide injunctions against the remaining policies of the Obama era—including Obamacare and environmental rules.

The Resistance has also done enormous damage to the reputation of the judiciary, in particular to the Supreme Court. Their flawed legal approach, their constant state of "emergency" (as Justice Thomas put it), has forced the high court to intervene again and again. Each intervention puts the Supreme Court in the hot seat and makes it even more controversial. The Court has had no choice but to step in and settle questions that lower courts have forced to the forefront. But Trump critics use each of these occasions to spotlight Trump's two Supreme Court nominees—Gorsuch and Kavanaugh—and to suggest all of the Court's conservative members are working as Trump's lackeys. Every one of these "faux" legal emergencies helps to chip away at the Supreme Court's authority.

Resistance judges begin from the position that Trump is operating outside of norms. The irony, as Blackman has noted, is that their reaction has been to operate even further outside norms. But it isn't the courts' job to judge Trump's behavior. Their job is to interpret the law. Judges don't get to ignore the rules simply because they loathe the president. And their decision to insert political animus into our judicial system is undermining American belief in a blind Lady Justice.

CHAPTER 9

AMBUSH

The Resistance repeated one name after the election with bitter regularity: Merrick Garland. Obama nominated Garland to the Supreme Court in March 2016, after the unexpected death of Justice Antonin Scalia. Senate Republican Leader Mitch McConnell refused to give Garland a hearing, citing the "Biden Rule." Joe Biden in June 1992 led the Senate Judiciary Committee, and he gave a speech in which he declared his opposition to considering any Supreme Court nominees in the run-up to a presidential election. McConnell adopted the same position, stating that the "American people" should "have a voice" in which president got to name Scalia's successor.

Trump's victory transformed the haters' anger over Garland into pure fury. And it pushed Trump's court nominations to the center of the Resistance effort. Outside activist groups mobilized to oppose each and every one of Trump's picks. They were joined by Senate Democrats and jointly unleashed an unprecedented campaign of smear tactics and ambush politics. This degradation of the Senate confirmation process culminated in the circus that was Brett Kavanaugh's nomination to the Supreme Court, an episode that South Carolina Republican Lindsey Graham would declare "the most despicable thing that I have seen in my time in politics." The country had seen ugly

Supreme Court battles in the past; "Borking" is a verb for a reason. But nobody had seen anything like this.

The haters wrecked much more than just reputations. Senate
Democrats forced Republicans to invoke the "nuclear" option to
kill the filibuster for Supreme Court nominations. They made
a farce of the nomination process and destroyed the informal
standards of the Senate Judiciary Committee. Members hid information from Chairman Chuck Grassley, broke committee rules,
and slandered their colleagues—setting an undignified new standard for future confirmations. Outside organizations like the
American Bar Association took blatantly partisan steps that undercut the role in the future for advisory groups in the nomination process. The Resistance further politicized the FBI, trying to
force it into a new job of passing judgment on nominees. Activist
organizations targeted individual Republican senators with extraordinary and ugly pressure campaigns. At one point, a Resistance
group even tried to bribe Maine Senator Susan Collins, offering
to trade political donations for a vote against Kavanaugh.

Overall, the speed with which Democrats rejected each of
Trump's picks did real damage to the integrity of the judiciary.
They cast aside all the traditional metrics that we normally use
to vet judges—intelligence, experience, reputation—in favor of
bald political criteria. That approach reinforces the dangerous
and growing public view that judges *are* political actors—
partisans who are incapable of fairly adjudicating legal disputes.
Nothing Trump has ever done as a candidate or in office has approached the damage these Resistance antics have done to the
judicial branch.

* * *

Neil Gorsuch, if anything, had it easy. Trump nominated the
49-year-old Coloradan to the Supreme Court on January 31,
2017. The nomination wasn't that big of a surprise. Trump had

added Gorsuch to his list of potential Supreme Court picks in September 2016, and by January, Gorsuch was known to be among the frontrunners.

Gorsuch was an inspired pick in part because he was so uncontroversial. He was a star on the Tenth Circuit Court of Appeals, where he was appointed in 2006 by George W. Bush. He was relatively young, brilliant, and known in legal circles for his crisp writing. His long paper trail—showing opinion after opinion that relied on textualist principles—was reassuring to conservative groups and GOP senators. Republicans had been sorely disappointed by prior Supreme Court picks like Sandra Day O'Connor and Anthony Kennedy, who had drifted left after their confirmations. Gorsuch looked sound, in particular on key issues like religious liberty, gun rights, free speech, and skepticism of the administrative state.

Democrats couldn't find anything of substance in Gorsuch's stellar legal record with which to bash him. He was bright, sober, and undoubtedly qualified for the Supreme Court. The left's frustration with this résumé spilled through in a speech by Senate minority leader Chuck Schumer in the run-up to Gorsuch's hearing. Schumer whined that even though Gorsuch "may act like a neutral, calm judge," and that "he expresses a lot of empathy and sympathy for the less powerful," he was in reality a judge that "harbors a right-wing, pro-corporate, special-interest agenda." And for a time, Democrats tried to run with that theme— claiming that Gorsuch too often ruled in favor of big companies. It was an asinine argument; judges are supposed to look at facts and law, not relative wealth or power.

Democrats' bigger problem was that the Gorsuch paper trail showed that he was, in fact, a mainstream conservative judge, known as a consensus builder. Jeff Harris at Kirkland & Ellis did an analysis of the 800 or so opinions Gorsuch wrote on the Tenth Circuit. Only 1.75% (14 opinions) drew dissents from his colleagues. Put another way, 98% of his opinions were unanimous, and on a circuit where 7 of the 12 active judges had been appointed by Democratic presidents.

Despite this distinguished record, the Resistance demanded Senate Democrats bring Gorsuch down. And they did try a late hit. In early April, *Politico* ran an article suggesting Gorsuch had once plagiarized a few sentences. But they were laughable examples, and even one of the academics Gorsuch had supposedly plagiarized came out to dismiss the claim as nonsense. In growing desperation, outside groups including labor unions and abortion activists sent letters to the Democratic leadership, demanding it filibuster Gorsuch and subject him to a 60-vote threshold.

This was unprecedented. Republicans weren't happy with an Obama presidency, and many Senate Republicans didn't like his nominees to the Supreme Court. Yet the GOP, which was in the minority at the time, never filibustered an Obama Supreme Court pick. Quite the opposite: Most Republicans took the view that Obama had every right to choose his nominees, and that the only question was whether they were qualified. Obama's first nominee, Sonia Sotomayor, was confirmed by a vote of 68–31 in August 2009. Obama's second pick, Elena Kagan, was confirmed 63–37 in August 2010.

Democrats were now in the minority, and before Gorsuch had even had a hearing, Oregon Resistance Senator Jeff Merkley called for his party to filibuster. And sure enough, in early April all but four Democrats voted against advancing his nomination to a final vote. It was an extraordinary new standard. A Republican president, duly elected, would no longer be allowed to install even a highly distinguished judge on the Supreme Court without 60 Senate votes. And Democrats would not provide any votes for anything less than a liberal judge.

McConnell had no choice but to go "nuclear" and get rid of the filibuster for Supreme Court nominations. Democrats had made this an easy call; Democratic Senate leader Harry Reid had been the first to attack the tool. He'd in 2013 eliminated the filibuster for lower-court nominees and Cabinet members, to make it easier for Democrats to confirm Obama picks.

The Democratic obstruction to a highly qualified nominee boomeranged on the party. McConnell's decision to get rid of the filibuster for the high court meant that Trump had more freedom in the future to nominate even more conservative judges. Moreover, the Resistance's unreasonableness united Republicans. The GOP Senate up to that point had been a hotbed of fractiousness. Republicans couldn't agree on Trump, on health care, on taxes. And more moderate GOP senators would normally have blanched at taking such an extreme step as nuking the filibuster. But the left had made clear with its antics that it intended to block *any* Trump pick to the Supreme Court, and Republicans understood that the only way to return the Senate to its more traditional "advice and consent" role was to go nuclear. Senate Republicans voted en bloc on April 6 to lower the threshold for ending debate on Supreme Court nominees to 50 votes. Gorsuch the very next day was confirmed 54–45. Only three Democrats were ultimately willing to vote for this most distinguished legal jurist.

To be clear: Democrats forced McConnell to abandon the Supreme Court filibuster. And to be clear, that move could have alarming consequences for the future. Trump's two nominees to the Supreme Court have both been eminently qualified, mainstream jurists. But the end of the filibuster makes it easier for a future president to nominate a radical, since it now takes but 50 votes for confirmation. Democrats claim to want the Supreme Court to be a moderating influence in the U.S. political system. But their actions continue paving the way for immoderation.

* * *

The Gorsuch confirmation galvanized the Resistance. Trump haters were livid that Senate Democrats had not done more to destroy the nominee. And the anger mounted as Trump announced a string of lower-court nominees, and McConnell's Senate quickly confirmed them. Resistance leaders began mobilizing their masses specifically around the courts. A *New York Times* piece in May 2018 about one of these efforts focused on a new organization—Demand Justice—created entirely to "instill" a "zeal" in "progressive voters on issues related to the federal judiciary." The goal was to inflame the liberal troops, to put extreme new pressure on Senate Democrats to obstruct or destroy Trump nominees.

The pressure helped further demolish Senate traditions. Democrats couldn't stop nominees; the filibuster was gone for all judicial appointments. But they could slow things way down. Senators began demanding cloture filings for every nominee— no matter how uncontroversial. That demand meant that each Trump pick—even after all the usual vetting and hearings— would be subject to a two-day waiting period and then thirty hours of debate. Democrats didn't actually show up to "debate" anything about the nominees—the cloture demands were simply time wasters. They had a side benefit for Democrats, too, in that they halted other business, slowing the GOP's policy agenda.

Minority parties have always had the ability to subject the chamber to such foot dragging, but in the past, cloture demands were used more as a negotiating tactic. In 2013, for instance, Senate leader Reid cut a deal with minority Republicans. He'd give them more opportunity to offer amendments to legislation, in return for Mr. Reid's ability to limit post-cloture debate for most nominees to eight hours. That deal let Reid confirm dozens of judicial nominations. But it expired in 2015, and Schumer, the new Democratic leader, now in the minority, refused to renew it. Democrats continued to use cloture for sheer and bloody-minded obstruction.

Democrats also put cloture demands on Trump executive nominees, including the most inconsequential of administration jobs. By April 2018, Democrats had demanded 128 cloture votes, including for the first time in history on 42 executive-branch positions. McConnell cited as an example the insane obstruction of Ronald Batory, Trump's nominee to the Federal Railroad Administration. Batory had worked in the industry for decades, and nobody opposed his nomination; he was ultimately confirmed on a voice vote, meaning no Democrat ultimately objected. Nonetheless Senate Democrats blocked him from getting that vote for more than 200 days. The over-the-top cloture demands ultimately provoked Republicans in April 2019 to unilaterally change Senate rules, limiting debate for most executive and judicial nominees to two hours.

Democrats also started refusing to return "blue slips" to the Judiciary Committee. Blue slips are a bipartisan tradition, a way for senators to object to judicial nominees from their home state. The blue slip system was designed to improve the nomination process, by allowing senators to use their knowledge about home state judges to better inform White House picks. But Democrats instead turned the tradition into a new form of veto over all Trump judges. They uniformly refused to return blue slips to the committee even for highly qualified nominees and insisted this meant that the Judiciary Committee could not proceed to a vote.

An early example of this tactic came from Minnesota Democrat Al Franken. He refused to return a blue slip for David Stras, a supremely qualified Minnesota Supreme Court judge whom Trump nominated to the Eighth Circuit Court of Appeals. Stras had earned the highest rating from even the liberal American Bar Association and, like Gorsuch, had a flawless legal record. Franken complained instead about the people Stras admired. He grumbled that Stras early in his career had "worked as a law clerk for Justice [Clarence] Thomas," and had also once spoken about how "the jurisprudence of Justice [Antonin] Scalia helped to shape his own views." Since when was admiring a Supreme Court justice a disqualification for the federal judiciary?

Liberals then went ballistic when Judiciary Chairman Grassley in late 2017 decided to proceed with Stras's nomination despite Franken's missing blue slip. They ignored the fact that few heads of the committee had ever treated it as an end to a nomination. Democrat Joe Biden, for instance, only required an administration to consult with home state senators, regardless of what later happened with blue slips. Republican Strom Thurmond gave a deadline for returning the slips and often proceeded whether he got them back or not. Grassley spent most of 2017 attempting to preserve the blue slip tradition. But when it became clear Democrats were using blue slips for obstruction rather than for quality discussion, he had no choice but to ignore them.

Democrats were proud of all this resistance, but they also created new practices that hurt the confirmation process and will hurt their own side at some point. Both parties should want the Senate actively engaged with the White House in judicial nominations, providing "advice"—as the Constitution envisions. By turning the blue slip into a cudgel, Democrats destroyed that line of communication. And Republicans will not forget this obstruction. A basic Washington rule is that parties build on each other's worst behavior—not their best. The next Democratic-led Senate may face even worse obstruction from a minority GOP. Americans are already frustrated that Washington is too often in gridlock. A Senate held hostage to permanent procedural obstruction is a Senate unable to do the people's work.

* * *

The Resistance got the news they'd been most dreading on June 27, 2018: Justice Anthony Kennedy was retiring after thirty years on the Supreme Court. The announcement sent Trump haters into meltdown.

As much as the Gorsuch confirmation rankled, it had also been a bit of a wash. Republicans had replaced one conservative Supreme Court Justice (Scalia) with another (Gorsuch). The

Kennedy retirement was something else entirely. Kennedy was a Reagan appointee but had become a fickle judge. The Court's swing vote, he joined liberals on the Court on big cases with almost as much frequency as he joined conservatives. Trump's nomination would guarantee a solid conservative majority, potentially for years to come. And Trump moved quickly, nominating 53-year-old Brett Kavanaugh on July 9, 2018.

Kavanaugh was another inspired pick, a model Supreme Court nominee. He'd gone to Ivy League schools; he'd clerked for Kennedy; at the time of his nomination he had already served for twelve years on the important D.C. Circuit Court of Appeals. Over that tenure he'd written more than 300 opinions, at least 10 of which had been upheld by the Supreme Court. And like Gorsuch, he was a mainstream conservative jurist. Of the many cases and orders that Kavanaugh took part in while at the D.C. Circuit, 97 percent of them were unanimous. As we at the *WSJ* wrote at the time of his nomination, Kavanaugh was "the center-right version of his colleague on the federal bench, Merrick Garland, whom Democrats continue to laud as an ideal Justice."

His nomination was nonetheless met with (predictable) hysteria. Progressive groups decried him as "extreme," "dangerous," and "outside the legal mainstream." U.S. Senate Democratic Whip Dick Durbin declared him a "far-right jurist" who would allow "the worst impulses of the Trump presidency" to go "unchecked." The Democratic National Committee claimed that with "Brett Kavanaugh on the bench, *Roe v. Wade*, affordable health care, labor unions, and civil rights will all be on the chopping block." The NAACP said a Kavanaugh confirmation spelled the end of "equal opportunity in education, employment and housing," as well as "further exclusion of communities of color" from "our democracy" and flourishing "racism" in the "criminal justice system." And within moments of Trump's announcement, Senate minority leader Chuck Schumer declared: "I will oppose Judge Kavanaugh's nomination with everything I have." Schumer hadn't even bothered to read Kavanaugh's record or meet with him. His declaration was proof that for Democrats this was not about legal qualifications; it was about thwarting Trump.

Schumer's promise wasn't enough for the Resistance, which in August made it clear that Senate jobs were on the line. By the end of that month, Democrats were raring to exit Washington and hit the midterm campaign trail. McConnell said nobody was leaving until the Senate cleared fifteen Trump judicial picks. Schumer made a deal to fast-track the confirmations, so that his people could get to their states.

The Trump haters exploded. Brian Fallon, the head of Demand Justice, went on the warpath. "Mitch McConnell is in the middle of stealing the federal courts for conservatives, and Democrats continue to bring a butter knife to a gunfight," he raged in a statement. "Democrats should be resisting Trump's judge picks at every turn, not agreeing to fast-track them, as happened this week. It is hard to think of a more pathetic surrender heading into the Kavanaugh hearings." Markos Moulitsas of the *Daily Kos* declared: "Democrats need a new Senate leader." Vox suggested Schumer's job was at risk, referencing a New York telephone town hall in which his constituents had "argued that Schumer lacked the teeth needed to truly take on the Republicans." Yet other liberal groups sent the message that all Democrats were expected to get tougher. As a *Huffington Post* story noted: "It would have taken only one Democratic senator to say 'no' to letting the nominees through this week, but none did."

The problem for Schumer and Democrats (as even some liberal commentators acknowledged) was that there was nothing they could do procedurally to stop a Kavanaugh vote. They'd exploded the filibuster for Supreme Court nominees in the Gorsuch fight, and McConnell had a 51-senator majority. Schumer had only two courses available to him. The first: Attempt to string out the Kavanaugh confirmation process past the November midterm elections. Democrats hoped to retake the Senate majority and put any court nominations on ice until they could win back the White House. This strategy would have the additional benefit of sparing Schumer's red-state Democratic senators from having to take a tough vote on Kavanaugh prior to their reelections. The second: Pressure at least a couple of Senate Republicans to abandon the nominee, denying him even 50 votes.

Democrats moved immediately to slow the process, demanding millions of documents from Kavanaugh's tenure as a staff secretary in the George W. Bush White House and from his time working for independent counsel Ken Starr. Schumer said he wouldn't even meet with the nominee until his document demands were satisfied.

This was unheard of. Reasonable document requests usually bear only on the duties of a Supreme Court justice. Kavanaugh's job as White House staff secretary made him the gatekeeper of a mountain of documents—few of which were created by him and even fewer that would bear on his qualifications to the high court. The Democratic demands were far in excess of anything administrations had been asked to provide for former nominees. Notably, while the Obama team had turned over some of Kagan's records from her time in the Obama White House, then–Senate Judiciary head Pat Leahy had not requested any documents from her time at the Obama Justice Department. Why? They were covered by executive privilege. But Democrats wanted to ignore that standard when it came to Kavanaugh.

When Republicans balked at the enormity of the request, Democrats started accusing the GOP of "rushing" the process and engaging in a Kavanaugh "cover-up." They blasted the GOP timeline, which was aimed at getting Kavanaugh confirmed in time for the Supreme Court's new term on October 1, 2018. That timeline was hardly a rush, providing more than 80 days for the confirmation process. By contrast, 60 to 70 days was the norm for previous nominees. But in mid-August, Schumer declared: "We are seeing layer after layer of unprecedented secrecy in what is quickly becoming the least transparent nominations process in history."

It meanwhile took less than a week after Trump named Kavanaugh for the Resistance to float its first smears against him—an early effort to make him too toxic for Republican support. It says something that the best the Trump haters could come up with was a claim of guilt by association. Kavanaugh, twenty-seven years earlier, had clerked for federal Judge Alex Kozinski on the Ninth Circuit Court of Appeals. Kozinski retired in December 2017 after several women accused him of harassing behavior. Resisters demanded that Senate Democrats grill Kavanaugh on whether he had any knowledge of these events. Their problem: He didn't. The Trump White House immediately issued a statement saying that prior to public reports in 2017 about Kozinski, "Judge Kavanaugh had never heard any allegations of sexual misconduct or sexual harassment by Judge Kozinski." And some eighteen of Kavanaugh's former female clerks signed a letter stating their "uniformly positive experiences with the Judge as a boss on issues of gender and equality in the workplace." The issue largely died, but was an early warning that the left (including the media) would abandon all its standards in the Kavanaugh fight and would be willing to level the cheapest and most scurrilous of accusations.

Democrats were ultimately provided more than half a million pages about Kavanaugh's record—more than had been provided for the past five Supreme Court nominees combined. They also had 17,000 pages of material that Kavanaugh provided in response to the committee's questionnaire. None of this counted for anything in the end. From the first minute of Kavanaugh's September 4 hearing, Democrats engaged in never-before-seen theatrics for the cameras—eager to please the progressive base. As we at the *WSJ* editorial page wrote: "Judiciary Chairman Chuck Grassley couldn't finish his first sentence before California Democrat Kamala Harris interrupted to demand a hearing delay.

Democrats continued to speak over the Chairman even after they were ruled out of order to the jeers of protestors who had to be removed from the hearing room. Democrats interrupted 44 times in the first hour, part of what NBC reported as a 'plotted, coordinated strategy' organized by Minority Leader Chuck Schumer over the weekend." Washington isn't the classiest place, but this was undignified to an extreme.

Histrionics over, Democrats moved to bashing the nominee. Ms. Harris claimed he would not be loyal "to the people of the United States." Democrats also claimed Trump had chosen Kavanaugh only to somehow save him from a Mueller indictment. This made no sense, since existing DOJ guidelines don't even allow indictments of a sitting president. They claimed he'd overturn Supreme Court precedents willy-nilly, that he'd act as a corporate stooge, and that he'd unleash a new wave of gun violence. The drama went on for four excruciating days.

It was capped by New Jersey Democrat Cory Booker's declaration that he intended to violate strict Senate rules and release confidential documents. Senators had been allowed to review some documents that had been marked "Confidential" and not made available to the public. Booker late in the hearings referred to one of these—an e-mail that Kavanaugh had sent while he was in Bush's White House counsel office that had the subject line "Racial Profiling." Booker went on a rant, claiming that the "system is rigged" and declaring he would release the documents in defiance of committee rules. "This is about the closest I'll probably ever have in my life to an 'I am Spartacus' moment," he dramatically declared.

Embarrassingly for Booker, the documents were already public at the time he made his statement. The Judiciary Committee had pulled an all-nighter to honor Booker's earlier request to get the e-mail out. Equally embarrassing, the e-mail was much ado about zip. In response to an e-mail thread discussing the legal question of racial profiling after the 9/11 terror attack, Kavanaugh had responded that he "generally" favored "effective security measures that are race neutral." Shocker.

* * *

Kavanaugh more than survived his hearings; he got through without any serious scratch. The Resistance nonetheless ramped up pressure campaigns on individual Republican senators, looking to erode Kavanaugh support. A top target was Susan Collins, a Republican moderate from Maine, a champion of abortion rights. Democratic complaints that Kavanaugh would overthrow *Roe v. Wade* were always aimed at Collins and fellow female Republican Senator Lisa Murkowski from Alaska.

But in August, Kavanaugh sat down with Collins, in a long meeting that the Maine senator described as a "good, thorough discussion." And Collins directly addressed *Roe v. Wade*, saying she'd been reassured. "He said that he agreed with what [Chief] Justice [John] Roberts said at his nomination hearing, in which he said it was settled law," reported Collins. The Resistance claimed Kavanaugh was lying and set about brutally changing Collins's mind.

Collins would later report that activists started leaving "out-of-state voicemails" on "the answering machines" of her state offices. Some were criminal. "In one case—and we are going to turn this over to the police, but unfortunately, of course, the person didn't leave a name or number—but they actually threatened to rape one of my young female staffers," Collins told the *WSJ*.

As the *WSJ* editorial page reported in mid-September:

The Senator's office also has been receiving coat hangers in the mail, a grisly attempt to insinuate that a Justice Kavanaugh would restrict abortion rights. About 3,000 have arrived so far. "I am pleased to say," Ms. Collins says with a small chuckle, "we had a group that has a thrift shop that helps low-income women ask us for 300 of the hangers. So at least 300 of them have gone to a very good cause."

This intimidation campaign culminated in an out-and-out attempt to bribe or coerce Collins. In September, a Resistance crowdfunding website asked donors to make a financial pledge to help give $1 million to Collins's 2020 opponent and to provide their credit card numbers. But the site explained: "Your card will only be charged if Senator Susan Collins votes for Kavanaugh's confirmation to the Supreme Court." In other words, the site was making clear that Ms. Collins would be able to avoid a well-funded opponent only if she voted the way they wanted. As of mid-September, more than 37,000 people had donated more than $1 million.

Again, as we as the *WSJ* wrote at the time: "Federal law defines the crime of bribery as 'corruptly' offering 'anything of value' to a public official, including a Member of Congress, with the intent to 'influence any official act.' The crowdfunders in this case are offering something of value—withholding funds from her opponent—in return for a Supreme Court confirmation vote." Collins told us that two attorneys had expressed their view to her that this was a clear violation of the federal bribery law; a third had said it was extortion. The senator, to her credit, was unbowed. In response to all this, she said: "I'm going to do what I think is right. I am going to cast my vote—as I have done on all of the other Supreme Court nominees that I've been called upon to consider—based on his qualifications, his character and integrity, judicial temperament, his record, and his respect for the rule of law and fidelity to the Constitution."

Again, Democrats had broken new and unseemly ground in their attempts to harass a senator into political compliance. The Senate has long been clubbish—which can sometimes have a downside. The upside is that the body has generally adhered to a higher standard of collegiality and respect than the House.

The Collins episode was notable for how few of her Democratic colleagues—even women—condemned these tactics. Democrats claim to want an environment of greater respect for women but encouraged an environment that led to attacks on Collins and sat back as political activists insulted a long-standing female senator in the foulest of terms. Try to imagine the uproar if a single Republican ever engaged in similar behavior.

* * *

In October 1991, news broke that a woman named Anita Hill had made allegations of sexual harassment against then–Supreme Court nominee Clarence Thomas. The allegations came but days before the Senate was scheduled to vote on his nomination. Many of her accusations were preposterous, and Pennsylvania Senator Arlen Specter would later write in his 2000 memoir that even Biden had admitted to him: "It was clear to me from the way she was answering the questions, [Hill] was lying" about a key part of her testimony.

Conservatives would later draw a comparison between this late hit on Thomas with the late hit on Kavanaugh. But as bad as the left's character assassination of Thomas was, its ambush of Kavanaugh was worse. And it brought the Senate confirmation process to a low that few could have ever imagined.

Remember the context: By mid-September, Kavanaugh was through his hearings and Democrats had failed to lay a glove on him. Republican senators seemed unmoved by the attacks. Yet Democrats as a whole remained under enormous political pressure to derail the nomination. And individual senators had personal motivations to take down the Republican nominee. Judiciary members like Harris and Booker were already gearing up for presidential runs and wanted to use Kavanaugh to prove their progressive bona fides. California Judiciary ranking member Dianne Feinstein was in the middle of a primary fight with a progressive opponent who claimed she was too soft. Democrats decided that if they couldn't destroy Kavanaugh on the question of legal competence, they would destroy him as a person.

The day before Grassley intended to mark up the Kavanaugh nomination to move it, Feinstein suddenly announced that she had "information." It was the slimiest of moves—an anonymous and ominous threat. "I have received information from an individual concerning the nomination of Brett Kavanaugh," said Feinstein in a statement. "That individual strongly requested confidentiality, declined to come forward or press the matter further, and I have honored that decision. I have, however, referred the matter to federal investigative authorities." Grassley immediately noted that Feinstein had failed to share the information with him. But someone *had* shared it with the media. News reports began claiming that Feinstein had a letter from a woman alleging Kavanaugh had engaged in sexual misconduct with her . . . in high school.

Everything about Feinstein's late ambush was improper. It turned out Feinstein had had the letter since summer. She hadn't sent it to the FBI, and she hadn't shared it with Republican colleagues. She also hadn't brought up the allegations when she met with Kavanaugh. Nor had she aired the issue during his official hearings. She instead waited until the formalities were over, then dropped it to derail his committee vote.

Within four days, liberal reporters had everything: Christine Blasey Ford claimed that when she was fifteen and Kavanaugh was seventeen, he and a friend pushed her into a bedroom at a party, held her down, covered her mouth, and groped her. She said she managed to escape.

Nothing about Blasey Ford's story added up. Kavanaugh denied it unequivocally. Reporters identified the "male friend," Mark Judge, who said he had no memory of the event. Nor did the fourth person Blasey Ford claimed to have been at the party— her good friend Leland Keyser. Blasey Ford, by her own admission, told nobody about this supposedly earth-shattering event until 2012—when she related the story during couples therapy. But even that was problematic. The therapist's notes said Blasey Ford claimed to have been assailed by four men, not two. Blasey Ford claimed the therapist was mistaken. The therapist's notes also never mentioned Kavanaugh's name.

As ugly as was the Thomas sabotage, he had at least been hit with specific allegations that he could refute. Blasey Ford's story was conveniently undisputable. She could not remember when the assault had happened. She could not remember in whose home she had been. She could not remember how she got there, or how she got home. All of this made it impossible for Kavanaugh to provide evidence to the contrary.

Democrats and the entire media establishment instantly erected a protective wall around Blasey Ford: She was a woman, a #MeToo confessor, and anyone who doubted her claims would be decried as a misogynist and an enabler of sexual harassment. Yet Blasey Ford's actions were hardly those of a political innocent. In the run-up to the accusation, she had dismantled all her social media, making it impossible to look back at her prior political views. She also retained as her lawyer Debra Katz, a notorious Democratic activist and Hillary supporter.

Democrats nonetheless got their desired outcome. Republicans almost immediately agreed to delay a confirmation vote and schedule another public hearing. We at the *Journal* editorial page warned that the goal was to force "Mr. Kavanaugh into looking defensive or angry, and to portray Republicans as anti-women. Odds are it will be a circus." We were wrong in that last regard. It was worse than a circus.

Having successfully delayed the Judiciary Committee vote, Democrats turned to delaying it even further. Schumer insisted that nothing happen until the FBI had thoroughly investigated the claims. It was an inappropriate request, as Schumer well understood. The FBI does do background checks, and Kavanaugh had been subjected to them over the years. But their purpose is simply to interview people about the character and qualifications of a nominee. The FBI doesn't make judgments about the statements it receives; it compiles information and sends it to elected officials. It's up to those officials to follow up.

The FBI most certainly doesn't exist to conduct criminal investigations into nominees, in particular over allegations that concern state (not federal) law. This was an abdication of the Senate's constitutional duty to make the final call on the fitness of judicial nominees. Democrats were putting the Bureau in an untenable position, further politicizing it at a time when it was already under fire for its actions during the 2016 election. They were demanding that unelected bureaucrats at the FBI act as political judges in a partisan dispute—a role no American should want law enforcement to have in judicial nominations.

In any event, the Judiciary majority staff had already moved to investigate, and it had as much power as the FBI. It was doing the right thing, offering Blasey Ford an opportunity to testify in private or in public, with the goal of providing enough information for senators to judge her story and then vote. Their problem was that Blasey Ford did not want to cooperate. Senate Republicans immediately requested that she and Kavanaugh appear before the committee. Kavanaugh said he'd appear anywhere, anytime. But Blasey Ford's lawyers kept giving Republicans the runaround, refusing to say if they'd show up. At one point, they claimed she had a fear of confined spaces, including airplanes, and so would need to drive across the country—which would push any testimony off for longer. Democratic staffers also refused to work with their Republican counterparts on the scheduling of calls to witnesses. All of this seemed purposely designed to delay proceedings.

The delays also provided time for Kavanaugh haters to gin up more unfounded accusations. Right before a new hearing that would feature both Kavanaugh and Blasey Ford, *The New Yorker* landed a story in which a woman named Deborah Ramirez claimed that at a party in their freshman year at Yale—thirty-five years earlier—Kavanaugh had exposed himself to her. Ramirez admitted she had needed six days of "assessing her memories" to feel confident of the incident. She conceded to being so drunk at the time that she was "on the floor, foggy and slurring her words." *The New Yorker* could not find a single other eyewitness who put Kavanaugh at the party. The *New York Times* separately reported it had interviewed several dozen other people but could not corroborate Ramirez's story. It also reported that "Ramirez herself contacted former Yale classmates asking if they recalled the incident and told some of them that she could not be certain Mr. Kavanaugh was the one who exposed himself." Kavanaugh declared it "a smear, plain and simple." It's worth noting that one of the authors of *The New Yorker* story was the liberal Jane Mayer, who had spent a great deal of her career attacking Clarence Thomas with Anita Hill material.

Then, star-crazed lawyer Michael Avenatti (who had also represented Stormy Daniels) released a third accusation. The only benefit of this claim was that it was so monstrous, so fantastical, that it served to put the Kavanaugh spectacle into better perspective. Julie Swetnick, a Washington-area woman, claimed that Kavanaugh and Judge in high school had been part of a group that routinely targeted young women for gang rape at parties. Swetnick claimed to have been a victim of this abuse, but that she had attended more than ten such events—thereby suggesting she continued to show up at parties where she knew she'd be assaulted. Kavanaugh correctly called it "from the *Twilight Zone*." Grassley, on the basis of information the committee compiled, would later refer both Avenatti and Swetnick to the Justice Department for a criminal investigation, claiming they had engaged in conspiracy, false statements, and obstruction of Congress.

Nonetheless, within hours of the Avenatti-Swetnick craziness, every Democrat on the Senate Judiciary Committee had called on Kavanaugh to withdraw. To Kavanaugh's credit, he refused, saying he would not be "intimidated out of withdrawing from this process. The coordinated effort to destroy my good name will not drive me out."

With its demand for Kavanaugh's resignation, the Resistance formally threw over one of the fundamental precepts of American society: due process. That helped to weaponize every sexual assault allegation and further polarize the country. Schumer at one point attempted to suggest that Kavanaugh shouldn't be accorded traditional due process, since this was a Senate confirmation and not a court of law. But that's inane. We as a country accord due process in every realm. As the *WSJ* editorial board wrote: Due process "holds for charges of scientific fraud, legal malpractice, or violating the standard of a professional society. It even holds, tenuously, for sexual-assault cases on most college campuses where at least an accuser has to meet a 50.1% 'preponderance of evidence' standard."

The Resistance made the argument that the accusations against Kavanaugh must be believed simply because they were made. And that it was up to Kavanaugh to prove his innocence. But this turns due process on its head. Americans are always innocent until proven guilty, and the burden of proof is always on the accuser. If we abandon this system, then anyone who makes an accusation, even on a whim, holds the power to destroy another's life. Those accused are also afforded the right to cross-examine their accusers, to question their claims. Yet Blasey Ford's lawyers and Democrats instantly moved to limit how and about what Blasey Ford could be questioned in her hearing with Kavanaugh.

Democrats would later come to see up close and personal the mistake of according Blasey Ford's accusations special privilege. Within a few months, the Virginia Democratic Lieutenant Governor, Justin Fairfax, was hit with decades-old allegations of sexual assault. In February 2019, Vanessa Tyson accused Fairfax of sexually assaulting her at the 2004 Democratic convention, while Meredith Watson accused him of raping her in 2000 when they were both students at Duke. As was the case with Blasey Ford, neither woman had corroborating evidence. Democrats at that point would rush to try to reestablish some due process norms.

But that was later, and Democrats in September 2018 turned the Ford-Kavanaugh hearing into one of the lowest moments in the Senate's modern history. I was in the hearing room that day, a guest of a Republican on the committee. I at one point glanced over to see that one of my closest seat mates was Alyssa Milano, the #MeToo Hollywood actress and advocate—and it gave the entire day a surreal, scripted feel. The mood within the hearing room was extraordinarily tense. Ford testified first, putting in a sympathetic but bizarre performance. She alternated between claiming not to understand the most basic questions, to answering others with technical lectures about neurochemistry. Asked at one point by Feinstein about how she could be so "sure" it was Kavanaugh, Blasey Ford responded that it had to do with "the level of norepinephrine and epinephrine in the brain that sort of, as you know, encodes—that neurotransmitter encodes memories into the hippocampus . . ." But the important point of her testimony was that she still couldn't recall key details and still couldn't muster a single witness to corroborate her claim.

Kavanaugh for his part was passionate in his defense of his innocence. He invoked his children and his parents in his opening statement, and was emotional in rejecting the accusations. He pointed out the significant number of former female colleagues who'd written that he had always treated them with decency and respect. He stated that any investigation would clear him. He pointed out the Democratic politics that were driving the assassination of his character. He called the process a "political hit" and a "circus."

Democrats in their questions flat out called him a sexual predator; they didn't even bother to use the word "alleged." They spent hours grilling him about jokes in his high school yearbook, and whether they were, in fact, secret codes for sexual assault. Nobody came out of the hearing with any more information than they'd gone in with. Instead, the nation watched the Senate embarrass itself, and Democrats destroyed the last semblance of honor in that body's "advice and consent" power. South Carolina Senator Lindsey Graham by the end was shaking with fury. When it came his time at the mike, he called the behavior of his counterparts the "most unethical sham since I've been in politics." And he laid out a warning to American voters. Looking across the dais at Democrats, he thundered: "Boy, do you want power. And I hope you never get it."

* * *

Most Republicans came out of the Kavanaugh hearing even more resolved to vote for his confirmation. They understood the consequences of a "no" vote. It would destroy due process, further weaponize sexual assault claims, legitimize the atrocious behavior of the Resistance, turn future nominations over to the mobs, and likely lose them a Supreme Court seat. It would potentially even lose them the Senate. Republican voters were furious over Kavanaugh's treatment and were now making his confirmation vote a litmus test on senators up for reelection.

Democrats instead put their focus on the few Republican holdouts—in particular Arizona's Jeff Flake. Flake the year before had announced he wouldn't seek reelection, and he'd become ever more the grandstander. He'd never been a fan of Trump's, and the Kavanaugh fight clearly conflicted him. He seemed torn between disgust over the process, and a desire to look #MeToo sympathetic. He hemmed and hawed, got chased into an elevator by a Resistance activist, released several tortured statements, and finally . . . split the difference. Flake agreed to provide the last vote to move Kavanaugh out of the Judiciary Committee. But he also succumbed to Democratic demands and said he wanted another FBI investigation before a full Senate floor vote. Alaska Republican Lisa Murkowski, who'd also been wilting under pressure, joined with Flake. Republican leaders agreed to a one-week FBI probe.

The probe would ultimately accomplish nothing. But it gave activists a last few days to produce more controversy. In waded the liberal American Bar Association, whose head, Robert Carlson, sent a letter to the Senate also calling for an FBI probe and further delay. The ABA remained bitter that the Trump administration had demoted the guild from its primary role in evaluating judicial nominees. It was long the norm for presidents to submit candidates to the ABA before making nominations official, which gave the group an effective veto. But conservatives grew tired of the ABA bias, which often resulted in low ratings for conservative legal stars. George W. Bush became the first modern president to announce his nominations publicly before the ABA could pass judgment. His reward was seven "not qualified" ratings during his presidency. President Obama restored the ABA veto, and his "not qualified" count was, of course, zero. Mr. Trump reinstituted the Bush policy, and already in two years the ABA had rated six of his nominees "not qualified"—a record.

The ABA's Standing Committee on the Federal Judiciary in August had unanimously awarded Kavanaugh its highest rating and expansive praise. But Carlson, a Clinton donor, saw an opportunity now to sandbag the nominee. Carlson's letter had the deliberate effect of making it sound as though the ABA was running away from its recommendation, even though Carlson wasn't on the standing committee and didn't speak for that body. Utah lawyer Paul Moxley, the ABA's Judicial Committee chair, felt compelled to write to the Senate Judiciary Committee to explain that Carlson's letter had not been vetted by his members, and that "The ABA's rating for Judge Kavanaugh is not affected by Mr. Carlson's letter."

Democrats also tried to use Kavanaugh's defense against him—claiming his passionate Senate testimony proved he did not have the "temperament" to sit on the Supreme Court. "Judge Kavanaugh did not reflect an impartial temperament or the fairness and even-handedness one would see in a judge," Feinstein tweeted. "He was aggressive and belligerent." The haters maintained that while it was perfectly acceptable to accuse a sitting judge of gang rape, drunkenness, and violence, Kavanaugh had no right to defend himself, no right to show any emotion. The media quickly picked up this theme, and liberals started pressuring the ABA to reopen its evaluation on "temperament" grounds.

The FBI probe turned up nothing and McConnell rightly scheduled a Senate floor vote. The Republican holdouts kept the nation guessing about their vote to the very last. Yet when the most influential of the undecided—Susan Collins—finally spoke on October 6, she riveted a nation. In one of the more impressive Senate floor speeches in modern history, Collins berated a confirmation process that had "hit rock bottom" and slammed the special-interest groups that had spread outright lies. One portion of her speech is worth quoting in full:

> Certain fundamental legal principles about due process, the presumption of innocence and fairness do bear on my thinking and I cannot abandon them. In evaluating any given claim of misconduct, we will be ill-served in the long run if we abandon innocence and fairness, tempting though it may be. We must always remember that it is when passions are most inflamed that fairness is most in jeopardy.

She reminded the country that the Senate's duty under the Constitution was "advice and consent," and this meant an analysis of Kavanaugh's competence to sit on the high court. She methodically and intelligently walked through his legal record on everything from health care to presidential powers to judicial independence. We at the *WSJ* editorial page wrote: "The speech was a U.S. Senator weighing a nominee's objective, known record against her own beliefs and politics. This, presumably, is the practical meaning of advice and consent." Only at the very end of this thirty-minute speech did Collins announce she would vote to confirm Kavanaugh. Minutes later, West Virginia Democrat Joe Manchin announced he'd also vote yes. The only Republican to bolt was the ever-confused Murkowski. Kavanaugh was confirmed the next day.

Not that the drama was over. Vicious in defeat, the Resistance moved to denigrate the entire court system. Feinstein tweeted that Kavanaugh's confirmation "undermines the legitimacy of the Supreme Court." Former Attorney General Eric Holder chimed in with the same sentiment: "The legitimacy of the Supreme Court can justifiably be questioned." These were radical words and an unnerving departure from American political norms. The last time the country overtly flouted the Supreme Court's authority was in the civil rights era, when states refused to abide by the high court's desegregation ruling in *Brown v. Board of Education*. That revolt led to violence and the mobilization of the National Guard. To put these extremist Feinstein-Holder claims in perspective, imagine if Trump were to tell his millions of followers that they did not need to respect the authority of the high court. He'd be accused of fomenting a civil war.

Democrats also started to claim that Kavanaugh had "lied" during his confirmation hearings; New York's Jerry Nadler, in line to run the Judiciary Committee if Democrats took back the House, vowed an investigation into Kavanaugh's "perjury." Booker suggested Democrats might commence impeachment proceedings against the justice. Does any of this strike most Americans as the political "norm"?

Democrats also chose to use Blasey Ford as a campaign prop for the midterms. That decision proved a double-edged political sword. Kavanaugh had certainly mobilized the Resistance. But as the ugly process ground on, it equally mobilized conservatives. They were used to their nominees getting harsher treatment but had never witnessed anything as revolting as the Kavanaugh teardown—and were enraged. Prior to Kavanaugh, Republican enthusiasm for the midterm election had been tepid. Post-Kavanaugh, it rivaled Democratic enthusiasm. The Democratic war on Kavanaugh not only saved the Senate for Republicans—it helped them add seats. Trump states took retribution on Democratic senators who voted against the nominee—throwing out Missouri's Claire McCaskill, Indiana's Joe Donnelly, and North Dakota's Heidi Heitkamp.

Things were tougher in the House. Many of the suburban districts Trump had narrowly won in 2016 had since soured on the president. Pelosi wisely recruited dozens of "centrist" Democrats for these districts, who ran on center-left platforms. The conservative energy that came out of Kavanaugh saved Republicans from the "blue wave" the pundits predicted. But it didn't save the House. Democrats made a gain of forty-one seats. Pelosi prepared to retake the gavel.

The assault on Kavanaugh was in many ways the purest expression of the motivations and tactics of the Resistance. Despite their claims, the haters did not oppose Kavanaugh on the basis of his qualifications, his temperament, or his history. While any nomination with the potential to change the direction of the Supreme Court would have been fiercely contested, the fact that Kavanaugh was Trump's choice teed the judge up for barbarous treatment. The Resistance, in its passion to block the president, set a new low in the nominations process, destroyed Senate traditions, and undermined the judicial branch. The damage will prove far more lasting than Trump's occasional jabs at individual judges or rulings.

CHAPTER 10

CRAZY HOUSE

On May 8, 2019, every Democrat on the House Judiciary committee voted to hold Attorney General William Barr in contempt of Congress. Judiciary Chairman Jerrold Nadler had less than three weeks earlier issued a subpoena to Barr, demanding he turn over to Congress the entire, unredacted Mueller report, as well as all of Mueller's underlying material, by May 1. Barr could not turn over the material without breaking the law. Federal statute makes it a crime to reveal grand jury material, even to Congress. The Justice Department offered to work with Democrats to get them as much material as possible within the confines of the law. Nadler instead abruptly shut down negotiations and moved to one of the quickest contempt votes in the history of the committee. Democrats *wanted* the contempt vote, to send a political message to its base that it was hammering the Trump administration. This was about the show, and it was yet another unfortunate abuse of power—done in the name of undermining Trump.

For all the Resistance's initial anger over Trump, it came out of the election lacking any real authority to do much about the new president. Trump had brought along both a Republican Senate and House. The GOP controlled both the executive and the legislative branches.

That changed on January 3, 2019, as Nancy Pelosi was elected again as Speaker of the House. South Carolina Senator Lindsey Graham had warned during the Kavanaugh hearings of the dangers of giving the Resistance "power." The country was about to witness the excesses firsthand.

We should take care not to include in that category of "excesses" the many things the 116th Congress has done that are completely normal. Republicans might not like Pelosi's many bills that seek to impose her progressive agenda. But House Democrats have every right to put any legislation they want through the usual committee order. House Democrats' refusal to provide Trump money for his border wall helped provoke the longest shutdown in U.S. history, but shutdowns aren't, sadly, a new thing. Republicans complain that Democrats are refusing to work with them on even bipartisan proposals, so committed is the Resistance to denying Trump any victory. But nothing says a House majority has to work with the other party. Voters will get their opportunity to judge this strategy in the 2020 elections.

The problem is instead Democrats who are turning the awesome powers of the House into partisan political weapons. The impeachment power is large and serious. Yet Democrats tossed the word around with as much regularity as they did the word "hearing," or "motion" or "bill." Holding an executive cabinet member in contempt of Congress is a serious move, yet Democrats slapped Barr with contempt in record time and for no reason other than to score political points. House Democrats have cast aside the usual rules on oversight—ignoring the traditional need to show true "legislative purpose" and instead demanding documents from Trump from before he was even in office. And Democratic presidential candidates promised to abolish the Electoral College, pack the Supreme Court, give sixteen-year-olds the vote, and confiscate existing firearms. Constitutional norms, anyone?

The thoughtless use of these powers has watered down their meaning, with alarming future consequences. Impeachment remains one of the only ways to remove a truly corrupt president. The more Democrats politicize it, the more wary future Congresses will be to embrace it when it is truly necessary. And Democrats' wanton threat of subpoenas and contempt citations has already made the Trump White House wary of complying with congressional demands. This destroys what in the past had been a tense but somewhat workable compromise—in which a Congress managed to see documents it truly needed for oversight, and a White House was able to protect those that went to the core of executive deliberation.

House Democrats in October 2019 voted for a formal impeachment inquiry over a conversation Trump had with the Ukrainian president. In December 2019 they voted for two articles of impeachment, claiming Trump had abused his power and obstructed Congress. Yet the Senate refused to convict, and more than half the country saw it as proof that Democrats were determined to reverse via brute force the results of the 2016 election. Again, nothing Trump has done compares.

* * *

Even in the minority, the Democratic Resistance didn't exactly cover itself in glory. Senate Democrats made a circus of the Kavanaugh hearing and abused their advice and consent duty with regard to Trump nominees. House Democrats used their perch to make libelous and unfounded accusations of treason and other criminal conduct. Committee Democrats in both chambers engaged in rampant leaking, stoking the press flames. Democrats sat idly by as Republicans attempted to wrest answers out of the DOJ about the FBI's 2016 behavior. Only when Democrats were back running the House did they suddenly decide that the bucking of congressional demands amounted to a "constitutional crisis."

In hindsight, House Democratic rule was destined to be wildly over-the-top. Democrats for two years had sloshed through the Resistance fever swamps, accusing Trump of every crime and transgression imaginable. Those Resistance voters were always going to demand that a new House majority act. The pressure from day one on Pelosi & Co. to take it to the White House was enormous.

The disappointment of the 2016 election had also energized the progressive movement. They blamed Clinton and the Democratic establishment for undercutting Bernie Sanders and then for blowing the election. They poured their frustration into the 2018 Democratic primaries, especially in more traditionally liberal districts. The Resistance fielded far-left candidates and propelled the likes of Alexandria Ocasio-Cortez (New York), Rashida Tlaib (Michigan), and Ilhan Omar (Minnesota) to victory. While centrists running in crucial districts won Pelosi the gavel, the Democratic House overall looked far more liberal after the election. New members from safe seats poured into the progressive caucus. Nate Silver's 538 blog pointed out in a November 2018 post that in 2010, there were about 1.5 progressives for every Blue Dog moderate in the House. "In 2019, the progressives will have a 4-1 advantage." These Resistance Democrats took office baying for blood and have consistently demanded the Democratic leadership bend to their demands.

Adding to this perfect storm: 2019 formally kicked off the Democratic presidential primary. Primaries are always about ideological purity; candidates cater to their party's base. But the base this time was a mob of progressive activists and Resistance types, and the 2020 candidates responded with ever more radical promises. Total renewable energy in a few years? Check. Forced licensing for all gun owners? Check. Government health care for all? Hell, yeah. This 2020 race also put pressure on the House to rival the anti-Trump enthusiasm of its top presidential contenders.

Finally, do not underestimate the power of ego. Republicans won the House in 1994, and save for the brief interlude of 2006–2010, they had run it ever since. Congressmen like Nadler were aching to hold the gavel and throw their weight around. The question was never what Democrats were going to do. The question was always: What wouldn't they do?

Democrats were careful not to flag their true intentions on the campaign trail. They knew it would turn off voters. Asked repeatedly during the 2018 election season if Democrats intended to immediately impeach Trump, Pelosi and other leaders repeatedly demurred. On the day of the 2018 election, Pelosi outright rejected impeachment. "I get criticized in my own party for not being in support of it," she told PBS's Judy Woodruff. "But I'm not. If that happens, it would have to be bipartisan, and the evidence would have to be so conclusive." Pelosi said that her interest was in everyday concerns. "They want to see us working to get that done for them. They want resolve. They want peace, and that's what we'll bring them."

Voters certainly got a lot from Democrats—just nothing peaceful. Before Pelosi had made it through her first full day as Speaker, California Democrat Brad Sherman, joined by Texas's Al Green, had formally introduced articles of impeachment against Trump for high crimes and misdemeanors. And Democrats were off to the impeachment races.

Impeachment, of course, has been used inappropriately in America's past. The House of Representatives impeached Andrew Johnson in 1868 over the president's defiance of a questionable piece of legislation (which was later repealed). The Senate failed to convict, the public viewed the proceedings as partisan, and what followed was a long period of bipartisan agreement to avoid the "I" word. In the modern era, impeachment proceedings were brought against both Richard Nixon and Bill Clinton—though in very different manners and with very different results. Republicans and Democrats jointly initiated impeachment proceedings against Nixon, giving the exercise greater solemnity. By contrast, many in the country viewed the GOP's unilateral impeachment of Clinton in 1998 as a partisan exercise, and they took it out on Republicans at the polls.

Both parties internalized that lesson, and it's why even prominent

Democrats continued to warn party leaders against moving on Trump. In 2018, longtime Obama adviser David Axelrod warned: "If we 'normalize' impeachment as a political tool it will be another hammer blow to our democracy."

Democratic leaders didn't heed his caution. The party spent much of early 2019 avoiding the topic by counseling everyone to sit tight, to wait for Mueller's findings. The party remained desperately hopeful the special counsel would hand it a clear and obvious argument for impeachment—one that even Republicans would struggle to deny. He didn't. Congressional Democrats, in demanding the special counsel, outsourced the legal questions of "conspiracy" and "obstruction" to the Justice Department. Once Mueller and Barr refused to bring charges, that should have been the end of it. Instead, Congressional Democrats wanted a do-over.

Or at least some did. In the wake of the Mueller report, Pelosi realized she had a problem. Half of her troops were still demanding impeachment; the other half feared it. Pelosi, at least initially, chose a middle option, which required an even worse abuse of House powers.

Democrats initially were reluctant to even hold a vote in favor of a formal impeachment inquiry—the first step of any true impeachment proceeding. Pelosi seemed aware that many Americans would view this as the real deal, and that Democrats would pay a political price. A *WSJ*-NBC poll in mid-May, following the Mueller report release, showed a scant 19% of independents felt there was enough evidence to launch an impeachment proceeding. The Pelosi Democrats in the spring of 2019 instead commenced what we at the *WSJ* editorial board labeled a "pseudo-impeachment." While they talked about impeachment incessantly and claimed the president was guilty of impeachment offenses, they refused to do anything official. This, as Axelrod worried, served to "normalize" impeachment talk, diminish its worth, and undercut democracy.

Even back in March, before Mueller had formally issued his report, Nadler, chair of the Judiciary Committee, went on ABC's
This Week to claim: "It's very clear that the President obstructed
justice. It's very clear. Eleven hundred times he referred to the
Mueller investigation as a witch hunt. He tried to—he fired—
he tried to protect [Michael] Flynn from being investigated by
the FBI. He fired [Jim] Comey in order to stop the Russian
thing, as he told NBC news." In response, *This Week* host George
Stephanopoulos asked Nadler the no-duh question: If Trump had
obstructed justice, a crime, why wasn't the House already im-
peaching? If he clearly obstructed justice, "then is the decision
not to pursue impeachment right now simply political?" asked
Stephanopoulos.

Nadler gave a non-answer about how he still needed to "do the
investigations" and "have the evidence all sorted out and everything," before proceeding to essentially *agree* with Stephanopoulos's point. "Before you impeach somebody, you have to persuade
the American public that it ought to happen," said Nadler. "You
have to persuade enough of the opposition party voters, Trump
voters, that you're not just trying to . . . that you're not just trying
to steal the last—to reverse the results of the last election." So
yes, this was political. Nadler was claiming Trump had committed a crime. He was also admitting that he intended to do nothing
about it until he could be sure voters wouldn't punish Democrats
for acting. If Nadler believed what he was saying about obstruction, he abdicated a constitutional duty.

More likely, Nadler didn't believe it. Constitutional lawyers
from former Attorney General Michael Mukasey to constitutional lawyer David Rivkin to current AG Bill Barr have
explained to Democrats a basic concept: Presidents cannot
obstruct justice when they are exercising legitimate constitutional powers. Those powers include the right to fire inferior
officers—including megalomaniacal FBI directors. They include
the right to berate special counsels (who also work for the pres-

ident). They include the right to advise on cases, as Trump did with Flynn. Presidents aren't allowed to commit a per se illegal offense, such as destroying or impairing evidence (acts that also wouldn't count as the exercise of an inherent constitutional power). But Nadler at the time of his "obstruction" rant had no such evidence.

Nor did Pelosi or any other Democrat, but that didn't stop the incessant impeachment drumbeat. A sampling of Pelosi's statements from just a few short weeks in March: "Trump is goading us to impeach him" (May 7). "He's becoming self-impeachable" (May 8). Trump "every day gives grounds for impeachment" (May 16). Yet Pelosi has also said that Trump is "not worth it," and that impeachment would be a "gift" to him. Which is it? These weren't the words of a serious elected leader, gravely wielding impeachment authority. The Resistance's slapdash and political approach to impeachment cheapened an awesome and serious tool.

The pseudo-impeachment, and the later formal impeachment, also led Democrats to overstep their congressional authority. The Constitution does not grant Congress an express right to conduct oversight. Congress's right to review, monitor, and supervise federal programs and policies is instead an implied right—and a clear one, given Congress's power to make laws and appropriate funds. But while Congress had broad authority to investigate matters, the Supreme Court has ruled that it must confine itself to "legislative purposes." This is why, for instance, Nunes did not conduct a wide-sweeping investigation of the Russia-collusion matter. His Intelligence Committee had jurisdiction over surveillance laws, and so focused on investigating FISA abuse.

Democrats began abusing their oversight powers almost immediately upon taking House power. A near-hilarious case in point has been House Ways & Means Committee Chairman Richard Neal's demand to see six years' worth of Trump's tax returns, from 2013 to 2018. I'm among those who wish Trump would make his records public. While it is not a requirement for the presidency, transparency in this area is generally a good thing. And while Trump undoubtedly worries Democrats will make hay over his finances, he's handed them an equally large weapon in their claim he is hiding something.

Either way, there is no law saying Trump must make his records public. And everyone understands Democrats want these in hopes of undercutting Trump's claims of wealth or to drum up some "financial fraud" charge. But Neal knew he needed a "legislative purpose" when he moved to obtain them. So he claimed, ludicrously, that his committee was "conducting oversight related to our Federal tax laws, including, but not limited to, the extent to which the IRS audits and enforces the Federal tax laws against a President." As for citizens' normal right to privacy in tax data, Neal cited a provision in the 1924 Revenue Act that gives the Chair of Ways & Means the right to review individual returns.

Trump Treasury Secretary Mnuchin refused, calling BS on Neal's contrived "legislative purpose." As critics pointed out, if Neal was truly interested in how the IRS conducts audits of presidents, he'd have taken an obvious first step: He'd ask the IRS how it conducts audits against presidents. He didn't. He simply demanded the Trump data. He also didn't ask for audit information regarding any other president—Obama, Bush, Clinton, etc. Most telling, Neal demanded information from the time period *before* Trump was in office. How does that have anything to do with auditing a president? It says something that Neal's demand was so flamingly transparent that Mnuchin felt free to preemptively declare he'd ignore the subpoena and see Neal in court.

Expect to witness many more lawsuits over "legislative purpose." Congresses and White Houses have long tussled over just which executive documents a legislature has the right to view. These fights usually end up in some form of a deal that balances executive privilege with congressional oversight. But Democrats have strayed so far from legislative purpose that the Trump administration by spring of 2019 was throwing up stop signs everywhere. By May, according to the *Washington Post*, Democrats were complaining that the administration had "failed to respond or comply with at least 79 requests for documents or other information." On the upside and in the long term, this could provide some further legal clarity on document production. But in the short term, the House Democrats' overreach is stymieing *legitimate* oversight. In their rush to tar Trump with "crimes," they are denying themselves the opportunity to provide effective, targeted oversight of key policies and programs.

Nowhere did Democrats abuse the subpoena power more than in their early, pseudo-impeachment proceedings. For starters, impeachment is only supposed to be a remedy for violations committed while in office. As Rivkin wrote for the *WSJ* in February 2019: "As Gouverneur Morris told the constitutional convention, impeachment would punish the president 'not as a man, but as an officer, and punished only by degradation from his office.' Alexander Hamilton likewise observed in Federalist No. 65 that impeachment involves 'those offenses which proceed from the misconduct of public men, or, in other words, from the abuse or violation of some public trust.'" Rivkin noted that the House in 1872 specifically chose not to impeach Vice President Schuyler Colfax for a pre-office action, because impeachment "should only be applied to high crimes and misdemeanors committed while in office."

Yet Democrats launched sweeping probes into all aspects of Trump's long life. The House Intelligence Committee under Schiff has sent out subpoenas looking at more than twenty years of Trump's business. Nadler separately sent out dozens of subpoenas, many for information that bore no relation to Trump's time in office.

Democrats arguably had no legal claim to many of the documents they demanded as part their follow-up Russia-collusion and obstruction probes. Many were highly sensitive documents covered by executive privilege; they included Trump's dealings with foreign officials, for instance. Others contained personal information.

Case in point were their sweeping demands that Attorney General Bill Barr turn over that completely unredacted Mueller report and all of the special counsel's underlying investigatory material. It was an extraordinary demand, especially given that Barr was obliged to turn over precisely none of it. The DOJ's special counsel regulations require the special counsel to file a "confidential" report explaining his "prosecution or declination decisions" to the attorney general. The AG has an obligation to notify the Congress only when he appoints a special counsel, when he removes a special counsel, and when a special counsel concludes his work. Barr was under no obligation to provide Mueller's report to Congress. In his confirmation hearings he nonetheless promised to be as transparent as possible under the law and regulations.

And within days of receiving the report, he had vowed to send Congress a version that contained only certain categories of redactions: grand jury information, sources and methods, information related to ongoing investigations, and details that might hurt the reputational interest of peripheral figures. The report Barr ultimately sent was only 10 percent redacted. And he immediately offered to make available to senior members of Congress an even less redacted version—only 1.5 percent was redacted material.

This wasn't good enough for Democrats, and on April 19, Nadler issued that subpoena to Barr for everything. But grand jury material is protected by federal law and restricted in its viewing public to government attorneys involved in cases. Congress is nowhere on the list of those entitled to access. Only

courts can grant Congress this information. Barr would have had
to break the law to comply with Democrats' subpoena. Unable
to accede to the subpoena's demands, Barr missed Congress's
deadline.

Democrats rushed to hold Barr in contempt, a criminal offense
that in theory allows a court to impose jail time and a significant fine.

* * *

Why the hurry? Mueller's report had handed Democrats an "obstruction" theme, and in the weeks following, Democrats
warmed to a new claim: Trump hadn't just obstructed justice, he
was obstructing Congress. Nadler's every interaction with Barr
looked designed to further stoke this narrative. Nadler claimed
that all he wanted was "evidence" as part of his "investigation" into
"abuses of power" by Trump. Yet every day Nadler did his level
best to ensure he did not obtain information.

He rejected, for instance, Barr's offer to see a less-redacted
report. At the time of Nadler's contempt vote against Barr,
not a single Democrat had visited the DOJ to look at the additional information. His subpoena meanwhile contained that
poison pill—the demand for grand jury information. Nadler
could have issued a subpoena that gained him tons of new material; he deliberately issued one that assured him none. In the
wake of the subpoena, Barr's office went into negotiations with
House Democrats, to try to find a solution. Nadler turned down
offer after offer. Justice offered to expand the list of Democrats
who could read the minimally redacted report, and even offered
to bring the material over to Congress. It also offered to accom-
modate prioritized requests for additional documents, based on
a committee review of the less-redacted report. Nadler said no
every time.

In the run-up to the contempt vote, Barr offered to testify in
front of Nadler. The Judiciary chairman deliberately attached an

unprecedented demand. He insisted that Barr be grilled by congressional staff members. No cabinet member had ever been subjected to such treatment in the Judiciary Committee's 206-year history, and Barr quite rightly refused. As Nadler presumably wanted. Nadler could have asked Barr all manner of questions; he purposely set the stage so that it wouldn't happen.

Most revealing was the rush with which Nadler held Barr in contempt. It was the opposite of how Congress normally obtains information. Republicans spent more than a year using contempt threats to pry documents out of the DOJ about the FBI's Russia investigation. They never got all they wanted, but they got a lot. Nadler's contempt resolution was the first step toward a protracted court fight, which could continue for months, if not years. It spoke volumes that Nadler chose that night after the vote to explain this most serious of contempt actions on that most unserious of Resistance cable TV slots—*The Rachel Maddow Show*.

Nadler played a similar game with senior White House advisers, including former White House Counsel Don McGahn and his chief of staff, Annie Donaldson. Nadler sent McGahn a subpoena in late April, demanding he appear to talk about episodes recounted in the Mueller report. The White House invoked executive privilege and ordered McGahn not to appear at the hearing. The White House Office of Legal Counsel also issued a memo pointing out that for more than thirty years, the executive branch had claimed absolute immunity with regard to testimony of close presidential advisers, and pointing out that even the Obama administration had taken that position.

As Nadler well knew, this is a legitimate point of contention. The Supreme Court has never clarified the question of whether presidential communication with advisers is entitled to absolute immunity. But some cases along the way have backed up White House claims that as a co-equal branch of government, neither the president nor those who closely advise him can be compelled to appear in front of Congress (just as a president cannot compel congressmen to appear at the White House). Yet Nadler refused to negotiate with McGahn or the White House about the boundaries of his testimony, or the timing, or the setting. And Nadler ignored the fact that McGahn was bound as former counsel to respect the office of the presidency and not testify. When McGahn failed to appear, Nadler also threatened him, and several other former White House advisers, with contempt proceedings.

The contempt votes were stunts—designed to further a Democratic narrative, not to send any serious message. None of those subject to the votes had, in fact, showed any real contempt for Congress; Nadler set them up to fail. This made a mockery of an important congressional tool, and at a time when Congress had been struggling with real questions about its authority and its lack of enforcement ability. The vote diluted the seriousness of contempt, making it more likely that future White Houses would flout even legitimate document demands.

And Resistance members made themselves look even weaker when—after the Barr vote—they dramatically called for House leaders to send the House sergeant of arms to arrest the AG. How concerned was Barr by this threat? At an event not long after his contempt vote, Barr walked up to Pelosi, grinned, and asked her if she'd brought her handcuffs.

Democrats had more claim to documents and witnesses when they finally voted for an official impeachment inquiry. Impeachment proceedings are viewed as a sort of court procedure, and judges tend to be more willing to grant congressional demands. But even here they managed to muddy the legal questions. Democrats were in such a rush to impeach Trump, they didn't bother to take the time to settle any of the access questions in court.

* * *

House Democrats went on to break every norm with their formal impeachment proceedings against Trump. And the 2020 Democratic presidential contenders made clear that was only the warmup for the next Democratic presidency.

The haters love to chant the fact that Hillary Clinton won "the popular vote"—even though it is a meaningless fact. The Founders put an extraordinary amount of thought into the Electoral College, and it is genius. The Electoral College is a recognition that we are a republic of fifty states. It's designed to require presidential candidates to earn support all over the country. It weeds out ineffective candidates, usually narrowing the field to two contenders, growing the likelihood that the final winner has a decisive victory—which increases legitimacy. And it speeds up election results, by turning over vote counting to the states. If you thought the 2000 hanging-chad debacle in Florida was bad, imagine sitting through a nationwide recount for the presidency. The Electoral College has endured for 230 years and hasn't missed a lick.

Yet in March 2019, presidential candidate and senator Elizabeth Warren called for its abolition. She complained that most presidential candidates do not routinely campaign in her home state of Massachusetts, since it isn't a battleground area. What she failed to note is that in a majority-rules system (as she favors) most presidential candidates wouldn't campaign in *most* states. They'd focus only on high-population areas. Warren would love nothing more than to have the residents of Boston, New York City, and Los Angeles pick our president every four years. Most of the rest of America wouldn't find this very American. Along with Warren, candidates including Kamala Harris, Beto O'Rourke, and Pete Buttigieg also expressed support for the idea.

Post-Kavanaugh progressives also adopted a new litmus test: that presidential candidates promise to forcibly change the Supreme Court to their liking. A new group called Pack the Courts wants a Democratic president to expand the number of justices, to put liberals back in the majority. Other Resistance groups are backing a proposal in which Republicans pick five justices, Democrats the other five—while the justices themselves pick five more "independent" members. (For the record, there have been nine justices since 1869.) The last time a president nakedly called to politicize the judicial process was in the 1930s. FDR, angry that the Supreme Court kept striking down his New Deal legislation, proposed a "court packing" bill that would have let him pick his own justices. The country was not impressed by his attempted end run of justice. Even his own Democratic Party was embarrassed and refused to move the legislation.

Yet Warren, Harris, Buttigieg, New Jersey Senator Cory Booker, and New York Senator Kirsten Gillibrand all called for changing the Court if they became president. At least getting rid of the Electoral College would require a constitutional amendment—a tough slog. The Court-packing provision could be done with simple majorities in both the Senate and the House.

When Nancy Pelosi suggested lowering the voting age to sixteen, Twitter had a field day. People started posting examples of their own sixteen-year-old judgment. "When I was 16, my friends and I bought a live lobster, put it on a leash, and walked it around the neighborhood at 2 a.m.," wrote one. "When I was 16, I sucked a drinking glass to my face for 10 minutes and gave my lower face a giant hickey that took 3 weeks to heal," wrote another. (These were quoted in a hilarious *Washington Examiner* piece.) Many people passed around the infamous video of the teenager who sets his buddy on fire while they attempt to do a cool skateboard stunt. And yet Democratic presidential contender Andrew Yang embraced the proposal. And 125 House Democrats voted for such a change in March 2019.

Here's what unites all the proposals: They aren't aimed at "fixing" a problem. Serious Washington people do discuss serious structural problems. An example is gerrymandering. Republicans and Democrats alike understand that gerrymandering is an issue. They debate it endlessly, and some states have moved to change the way they carve up voting districts.

These Democratic proposals are not about improvement; they

are about power. A majority-rules voting system would not be more "fair"; but it would undoubtedly ensure a Democratic president for decades to come. Few parents would ever advocate giving their muddle-headed teenagers the right to vote; Democrats only want it because they know the young are more susceptible to liberal, utopian ideals and would help guarantee them permanent congressional majorities. Question: What is the difference between thirteen Supreme justices versus nine? Answer: the person who gets to appoint them. Warren claims more justices would depoliticize the Court, but note that she isn't suggesting that change come *right now*. Quite the opposite. If Trump announced that *he* intended to expand the Supreme Court and appoint another six conservatives, Elizabeth Warren would call it the end of the Republic. The only things that bind these proposals together is a liberal fury over its losses and a liberal attempt to ensure its side has permanent control. This mirrors the approach of the crazy Pelosi House. House Democrats voted for vague articles of impeachment—"abuse of power" and "contempt of Congress"— that could easily be used against any future president, over any political disagreement. They used contempt against officials for failing to comply with impossible demands. These actions cross a Rubicon. They turn impeachment and contempt into partisan and political weapons, when both were designed to be serious tools for imposing accountability in grave circumstances. Where will a future Congress take this? It will get worse, not better.

One further observation: As Democrats released their proposals to demolish the U.S. system as we know it, a funny thing happened. The same media outlets that had spent the prior two years lambasting Trump for undermining the "norms" of governance applauded the Democratic contenders for thinking so far "out of the box." They also labored to explain why these Democratic proposals—which would overthrow our traditional system—had legitimacy and merit. Surprise, surprise.

CHAPTER 11

PRESS GANG

I've never engaged much in media criticism, for two simple reasons.

First, it's almost too obvious. Yes, the mainstream media is liberal. Always has been. And—just as important—always will be. Mainstream journalism tends to attract do-gooders who are out to save the world. Researchers from Arizona State University and Texas A&M University in 2018 surveyed 462 financial journalists. More than 58% admitted to being "very liberal or somewhat liberal." Another 37% described themselves as "moderate." Precisely 4.4% said they leaned right of center.

More important, journalism tends to attract people who all come from the same walk of life, attend the same schools, live in the same neighborhoods, and share the same worldview. This latter point is what is really behind "bias." I've worked in journalism now for twenty-five years, alongside many good news reporters. I can honestly say that I can count on one hand the number who were overt partisans and who knowingly used their positions to advance political views. Bias comes from something worse: insularity. Most reporters don't even know they are biased; everyone they socialize with holds the same left-of-center views. For all our modern talk of the need for more "diversity," newsrooms continue to ignore that which would provide the biggest benefit to their coverage: diversity of viewpoint.

Second, media criticism never gets you far, because it is so sub-jective. Conservatives can spot media bias from a mile away, in terms of the type of stories a newspaper or cable station runs, the language, the people they target, the "analysts" they employ. But those newspapers and stations always have an argument for why they did what they did. It was an important subject. It was a fair description. We ran something similar to this about the other side fifteen years ago, on page 37B. And look, we quoted one conservative. See? We are all about presenting both sides.

It is nonetheless impossible to ignore media problems in the age of Trump. Not because of press bias—which admittedly has become extraordinary, overt, and shameless. The Washington press corps is almost uniformly part of the Resistance; it hates Trump, no longer bothers to hide it, and works every day to undermine his administration. That's clear.

What's a bigger problem has been the press's willingness to *act* on its bias. The past few years have seen the greatest disin-tegration of press standards in modern history of the industry. The media has published evidence-free accusations, a new and alarming low. It has sourced its stories from people with clear political axes to grind, even as it has worked to hide those motivations from its readers. It's run with flamingly incorrect pieces and never bothered to acknowledge the errors. It has acted as a scribe for government agencies, dictating their version of events—a position that once would have earned reporters industry-wide shame. Most corrosive of all, it has closed its eyes to clear abuses, because those abuses do not fit with their anti-Trump narrative. This isn't bias; it is the destruction of press norms. Does Donald Trump fan the flames with his attacks on the press as "fake" and an "enemy" of the country? Sure. But the media has done a bang-up job all its own of providing Americans good reason to distrust it.

Add to this the financial benefit many media outlets have realized in presenting Trump as deranged. Ratings and revenues in the initial few years of Trump were nothing short of fantastic.

Russian "collusion" stories and impromptu Trump press confer-
ences were a godsend for a media industry that had at times
been struggling. Television ad revenues held steady, even as
many Americans cut the traditional cable cord. Newspaper subscriptions went up, despite reader dislike of having to pay for
subscriptions. The media understands that the juicier and more
outrageous the story, the more the clicks, views, and revenue.
And Trump is juicy stuff.

Yet it has had terrible consequences for the industry and for
the country. Gallup since the 1970s has been tracking American
trust in the media, which reached a high in the mid-1970s following Watergate reporting. In 2016, U.S. opinion that the media
reported news "fully, accurately and fairly" hit an all-time low—
32%. It was an eight-point drop from just the year before. (It
has since crept up but remains well below what it was in the
1990s.) And for the record, that approval rating was significantly
lower than Donald Trump's. In Gallup's 2018 poll, only 21% of
Republicans reported trust in the media, compared to 76% of
Democrats.

Meanwhile, a Monmouth University poll in early 2018 found
that a whopping 77% of Americans believe traditional TV and
newspaper outlets report "fake news." And 42% of respondents
said they believed outlets did this specifically to promote a political agenda. These kinds of numbers are alarming for civil society.
The press is supposed to play an integral role in holding officials
to account and helping the public make informed decisions. The
more Americans are turned off from traditional news, the more
they turn to social media and other truly dubious sources of information. It also creates a world in which Americans self-select
their news sources, meaning they increasingly read or listen to
only things with which they agree. America is growing more radical and polarized, and the press in recent years has played a big
role in that change.

* * *

A truly dogged media critic would need an entire book just to catalog the media meltdown that started in the run-up to the Trump presidency. For the point of this chapter, it's enough to provide a few key examples of how the press abandoned basic standards.

One particularly huge mistake helped drive all the rest: The press became willing advocates for government officials and agencies (at least the ones they liked). This is the reverse of the role the press is supposed to play. The media exists to be a government watchdog; the public depends on it to expose corrupt behavior.

When it has come to Trump administration actions, the press has done that with great energy, riding herd on every fact and issue. But when it has come to former Obama officials (Comey, Clapper, Brennan) and FBI and DOJ whisperers, they have served as willing scribes. They not only swallowed everything they were told, they also fought on those officials' side. It's hard to explain just how big a dereliction of duty this is. Reporters learn on day one that government officials exist to spin and lie, and that they do so with impunity. And the FBI's Trump-Russia investigation fell so clearly into the government-abuse-of-power stories that the press usually exists to expose—spying on a presidential campaign, wiretapping U.S. citizens. That story also came laden with facts that the press would normally view as glaring red flags—opposition research from the rival campaign, backdoor channels at the DOJ. And yet anything the people in power told it to write, the press wrote.

The best example is that infamous *New York Times* "origin" story. When Nunes finally looked about to win his battle with the DOJ to see the dossier documents in January 2018, the FBI protectors panicked. They knew how terrible it would look that they had used oppo-research from the rival campaign to spy on a Trump person. So someone called the *New York Times* for help in getting ahead of the story. On December 30, 2017, it published: "How the Russia Inquiry Began: A Campaign Aide, Drinks and Talk of Political Dirt." The story was, of course, all about how George Papadopoulos had inspired the FBI's probe, and it flat-out narrated what would become the Comey-McCabe line. It also flatly dismissed the dossier. The Papadopoulos tale "answers one of the lingering mysteries of the past year: What so alarmed American officials to provoke the F.B.I. to open a counterintelligence investigation into the Trump campaign months before the presidential election? It was not, as Mr. Trump and other politicians have alleged, a dossier compiled by a former British spy hired by a rival campaign." The *Times* cited nobody in its story other than anonymous "American and foreign officials."

Yet it would later come out that someone wasn't being honest about the dossier to the *New York Times*. The paper ran another "blockbuster" story in May 2018 about the FBI's Trump investigation, which was code-named Crossfire Hurricane. The *Times* reported that "Only in mid-September, congressional investigators say, did [the dossier] reach the Crossfire Hurricane team." This was false. Bruce Ohr would later testify under oath that he told everyone about the dossier—and its provenance—not long after Steele handed it to him in late July. As of this writing, the *Times* has never updated or corrected that piece.

* * *

The willingness to be spoon-fed is meanwhile what drove the many big press bloopers of the period. Reporters are only human and they make mistakes, but usually they are small things that are the result of sloppiness or speed. These errors were something different. Their entire premises were wrong.

Were there a Collusion Press-Error Hall of Fame, CNN would be the first inductee. There was CNN's decision in 2017 to run a story, based on one unnamed source, claiming a presidential adviser, Anthony Scaramucci, was under investigation for his ties with a Russian investment fund. CNN had to retract the story, and offered an apology to Scaramucci. Three of CNN's journalists resigned.

In December 2017, CNN announced a scoop for the ages. It claimed it had evidence that Donald Trump Jr. had been offered by e-mail advance access to hacked Democratic e-mails. MSNBC and CBS also claimed to have "confirmed" this evidence that the Trump campaign and WikiLeaks had been colluding over the hacked e-mails. It later came out that the CNN and MSNBC sources had gotten the date on their evidence wrong. Trump Jr. had been sent an e-mail directing him to look at the WikiLeaks dump—*after* WikiLeaks had made it public.

Or there was the July 2018 CNN report that one-time Trump attorney Michael Cohen was going to tell Mueller that Trump knew in advance about that infamous Don Jr. meeting at Trump Tower with Veselnitskaya. This would have made President Trump a liar, as he had already claimed no advance knowledge. CNN claimed that one of Cohen's attorneys, Lanny Davis, had declined to comment. Only, whoops! Turns out one of CNN's sources *was* Lanny Davis. Davis then admitted that he'd been mistaken about his information. CNN refused to retract the piece, claiming it was confident in its other sources. Yet the Mueller report never claimed that Trump Sr. knew about the meeting.

Also don't forget BuzzFeed's epic "news" in January 2019 that President Trump personally directed his longtime attorney Michael Cohen to lie to Congress about the Trump Tower project in Moscow, in order to obscure his involvement. Several politicians seized on this to hammer Trump. Schiff promised to do what was "necessary" to find out if the president had committed "perjury." Connecticut Senator Chris Murphy called on Mueller to immediately inform Congress. Democratic Representative Joaquin Castro said that if the allegations were true, Trump "must resign." The problem? They weren't. This one was such an invention that the Mueller team made a rare statement, outright denying the BuzzFeed report.

There were plenty more. The *Washington Post* claimed Russians had accessed the U.S. electrical grid through a Vermont utility. Not true. *Slate* claimed a Trump server had been communicating with Russia. Not true. The *Guardian* claimed that Paul Manafort had visited Julian Assange in his hideout at the Ecuadorian Embassy in London—not once, not twice, but three times. If so, Mueller missed it.

Aside from occasional scandals of reporters deliberately fabricating stories in order to advance themselves, nothing in recent years compares to this level and frequency of misinformation. The press gets furious when Trump talks about its "fake news." But what else would you call it?

* * *

Another low of the past few years has been the media's willingness to run fact-free accusations. Case in point: claims from the dossier. The specific charges in that document have never been proven. As I noted earlier, Fusion GPS was clever in that it fed the document first to the FBI, to give it more credibility with the press. But the fact the FBI had it, or that Representative Adam Schiff quoted from it in public, didn't release the press from a basic obligation: to either verify the truth or treat the document for what it was—slander. Instead, the media repeated the dossier's claims (Carter Page met with shady Russians, etc.) ad nauseum, barely bothering to note that they had not been proven.

This willingness to cast aside facts in favor of theory is what fed three years of hysterical collusion conspiracy theories. By embracing hypotheticals (rather than tracking down facts), the press indulged in endless "connect the dots" exercises. Liberal opinion writers were even worse. One of my all-time, laugh-out-loud headlines from 2018 came from Jonathan Chait, writing in *New*

York magazine. It read: "Prump-Tutin: Will Trump Be Meeting with His Counterpart—Or His Handler?" Chait asked: "What if Trump has been a Russian asset from 1987?" Then followed thousands of words that purported to tie together Trump, obscure Russians, Stormy Daniels, Julian Assange, and so much more. The story, suffice it to say, did not age well.

The dossier was the example of a dirty new trick the press would employ anytime it wanted to spew out unfounded claims. It would write (accurately!) about the "process" rather than the (inaccurate!) substance, using an FBI tip as an excuse to run unproven claims. For instance, in January 2018, two McClatchy reporters ran the following headline: "FBI Investigating Whether Russian Money Went to NRA to Help Trump." The story cited only two unnamed "sources familiar with the matter." The article admitted it "could not be learned" whether the FBI had any actual evidence involving the NRA. What mattered was only that the FBI was "investigating it." Other media outlets followed, and congressional Democrats started demanding that the NRA account for itself. The NRA flatly denied the slur (and no evidence of this claim was ever found).

The same two reporters in April 2018 would cite "sources" who said, "Mueller has evidence [Michael] Cohen was in Prague in 2016, confirming part of dossier." The story claimed Cohen had secretly snuck into the Czech Republic, through Germany, presumably for a clandestine meeting with Kremlin officials. It again quoted only "sources familiar with the matter." Yet Cohen had vehemently insisted he'd never been there. And the Mueller report would later flatly say he had not. McClatchy as of the writing of this book still hasn't retracted the story. Why? It claims that what it was reporting was that Mueller had "received evidence," and it noted that Mueller never said he didn't receive evidence. See?

Things were just as standard-free in the Kavanaugh battle. First came the smear stories questioning whether Kavanaugh had known about Judge Alex Kozinski's dealing with women twenty-seven years earlier. The stories were wild speculation and based on a memo from a radical leftist organization. The press then went crazy with Blasey Ford's accusations, despite the fact she had no proof.

And yet some newspapers seemed always able to rediscover their standards when it came to Democrats. In early 2019, Virginia Democrats were rocked by a claim by a woman who said Lieutenant Governor Justin Fairfax had sexually assaulted her in 2004. It later came out the woman had approached the *Washington Post* with her claims more than a year earlier, but the *Post* had chosen not to run her story. The newspaper would later explain that it did not publish because its reporters could not find anyone to "corroborate the woman's account." If only that had been the *Post*'s standard with Kavanaugh.

* * *

Finally: sourcing. Journalists don't just have an obligation to have quality sources; they have an obligation to cite them correctly. It's the only way the reading public can itself get a sense of the worth or motivation of the source. An accusation coming from a "career intelligence operative" will be viewed by a reader with far more weight than the same accusation coming from a "congressional Democrat."

Journalists know this, which is why we have the new fad of obscuring sources to the point of uselessness. Exhibit A was the lead paragraph of a *New York Times* story on April 3, 2019. It came in the wake of Barr's summary about the Mueller report, just as Barr was about to testify in front of Congress. It read: "Some of Robert S. Mueller III's investigators have told associates that Attorney General William P. Barr failed to adequately portray the findings of their inquiry and that they were more troubling for Mr. Trump than Mr. Barr indicated, according to government officials and others familiar with their simmering frustrations."

Let's unpack this. Apparently, "some" of Mueller's "investigators" told "associates" of their thoughts. How many is "some"? Mueller had a team of dozens upon dozens. Was it two? Or twenty? And who are the investigators? Were they lead attorneys? Or were they the guy tasked with doing a LexisNexis search? And who are the "associates"? Other people on Mueller's team? Old friends from college? As for those "government officials," which branch are they in? Were they part of the administration? Or were they . . . the partisan Adam Schiff? And also, what the heck is an "other"? A reporter? A former official? Someone's mother?

The point is that with such vagueness, it would be entirely possible to craft another, totally plausible lead. Something like: "A couple of extreme partisans on Mueller's team really dislike Barr, and they told Comey, Brennan, and the boys at Fusion GPS that they were unhappy, and those people told us here at the *New York Times*." Doesn't exactly pack the same punch, now does it?

Pro tip: Anytime a reporter is broadly citing a "government official," a "U.S. official," or an "American official," it is probably because that reporter is hiding a bias. Reporters do at times need to fuzzy up the specific job of a source. If as a reporter you were to acknowledge that your source was, say, one of three appointed officials in a department—you'd probably be blowing someone's cover. But enlarging a source universe to all of Washington is problematic.

So is willingly using sources who have axes to grind and not alerting readers to their motivation. This was a particular problem in the Russia story, thanks to all those "former official" references. Presumably, some of these "former officials" were the very people accused of abusing their FBI-DOJ power—or supporters of those accused. They had everything to gain from crafting a narrative. To quote this crew as an unbiased source of information—as simple "federal officials with knowledge" of matters—is irresponsible. It's a bit like anonymously quoting Al Capone as an authority on tax law.

Another example: *Politico* reporter Natasha Bertrand has from start made clear she is closely tied to Fusion GPS. She tweets about Fusion a lot and sometimes quotes a "source close to" the organization. In the spring of 2019, as DOJ inspector general Michael Horowitz prepared to issue his report on the FBI's 2016 Trump-Russia actions, Bertrand ran a story headlined: "Post-Mueller Report Likely to Target Russia Dossier Author Steele." It was partly a hit job on Horowitz—who has a sterling reputation in Washington. It quoted "several people interviewed by the Inspector General's office," including "former U.S. officials." These vague former officials were "skeptical about the quality of his probe." According to the anonymous cites, Horowitz wasn't "well-versed" in basic DOJ things like FISA warrants. Which is hilarious, given that Horowitz had at this point been the DOJ inspector general for seven years. The story also presented Steele in the best possible light. For an unknowledgeable reader, the piece might throw shade on the inspector general. For well-versed reporters and readers, the story read like a blatant favor to the Fusion crowd.

* * *

All reporters sometimes bend a rule; they obscure a source more than normal or go out further on a limb. But the important thing is that they usually do this in aid of getting *truth* to the public. What defined the media breakdown that started in 2016 was their destruction of standards in aid of peddling a fiction—the Trump-Russia collusion narrative. Think how far we have come from the days of Walter Cronkite's sign-off: "And that's the way it is." Today's "news" is instead about the way reporters "want it to be." Trust lost is not easily regained. The country needs a fair and balanced press; post-Trump, how does the industry ever gain that trust back?

CONCLUSION

For every Resistance leader who daily makes an inflated claim about Trump's destruction of democracy, there is a more quiet, average American who is deeply alarmed by the *legitimate* and *lasting* harm this movement is causing. When I go out on the road to do reporting or to give speeches, the most frequent question I am asked by this silent majority is: What can be done?

As with everything with politics, that's a hard one. The reality is that so long as Trump is president, the Resistance will continue. This puts a lot of 2020 voters in a difficult position. We'd like elections to be solely about policy. But with Trump, it is inevitably about the person. Many voters, even those who approve of Trump's agenda, are tired of the circus and tempted to bring it to an end by voting Trump out of office. Just as many are worried that a Trump defeat in 2020 will prove a vindication of the Resistance tactics and legitimize more such behavior going forward. None of this is about the issues, but it is a reality.

Some of the Resistance behavior of recent years requires a legislative or administrative response. Congress needs to revisit its surveillance laws, to make it harder for intelligence officials to misuse them for political purposes. It needs to clarify that law enforcement must notify it of sensitive investigations, so that lawmakers can ensure agencies are not abusing their powers. And it needs to consider abolishing the FISA court, which is a tool that elected and appointed leaders use to dodge accountability for their own actions.

The Department of Justice needs to reinforce its regulations and develop a better system for holding accountable employees who break the rules. Its leadership needs to re-instill in prosecutors and FBI agents the principle that the law isn't solely about throwing people in jail; it's about wielding powers with humility and also protecting the innocent. The legislative and executive branches need to work together to reform civil service laws and restore to the bureaucracy a merit-based system—in which those who perform admirably are rewarded, while those who misuse their positions are disciplined or fired. The Supreme Court needs to send some serious rebukes to the lower courts, to get judges back in line.

But what about the politicians who act out of bounds? What to do about them? There is an answer—for both the short and the long term. It isn't immediate, and it won't satisfy the impatient. But it does rest on a tried-and-true American trait: engagement.

American consumers are among the most picky, demanding, and irascible in the world—a national characteristic for which I have nothing but admiration. As a young adult, I lived in England. Nothing drove me crazier than the resigned attitude the Brits had to poor service. Their National Health Service treats average people with benign neglect, yet the citizenry is too used to this injustice to rebel. Service providers abuse their customers and consumers complain endlessly about the treatment, but they don't *do* anything about it.

Americans are the opposite. If they don't like a doctor, they get a second, third, or fourth opinion. Generations of Americans still scrutinize their diner bill down to the last penny and put serious thought into what percentage (if any at all) to tip a waitress. If a car dealer sells an American a lemon, you can bet that American will show up every day until he or she gets a fix. And while I have real issues with many class-action lawsuits, they are nonetheless another expression of American insistence on accountability.

Part of this is because the pocketbook remains king in our country, and that's a good thing. We care deeply when someone sells us a bum toaster or overcharges for gutter cleaning, or when an employee takes advantage and doesn't show up for work. These hurt our bottom line, and we feel it.

Politics is easier to ignore, since it is removed from our day-to-day. And people fear they are just one voice among many. But accountability works the same way. For too many Americans, politics is something we gripe about at night after the news program and vote on occasionally. A functioning civil society needs a much higher level of engagement. We need to be just as picky and just as demanding about our political outcomes as we are about our toaster, gutters, and employees.

A lot of Americans look at the federal government and feel it is a lost cause. It is so far away, so removed from everyday life. And in some ways that is true. Which is why I always remind people to start at the place the Founders intended them to start: locally. Do you know who sits on your school board? Do you know who your mayor is? Do you know who your state House representative or senator is? Find out. Find out what they are pushing. Go to the meetings, write letters, attend town halls, and hold them to account.

This engagement in local politics matters—it gives you more control over how your kid is educated, how often the trash is picked up, and how your property tax dollars are used. But it *does* also play into national politics. Local leaders are the farm team for higher office. The more they are expected by their constituents at lower levels to respond to demands, the more responsive they will be as they move up the ranks. Too many Americans put untested and unproven candidates into positions of serious consequence. And we are witnessing what happens when the unserious are allowed to run the country.

By all means, also engage at a national level. If you are unhappy that Resistance leaders are abusing the impeachment process, or refusing to hold FBI leaders to account, or giving bureaucrats a pass on inappropriate behavior—say so. Call, write, show up at their state office. Let them know how unhappy you are. You might think that one voice is nothing. But you aren't one voice. Millions of Americans feel the same fervor about keeping our country on a strong, viable, constitutional path. All those voices together cannot be ignored.

ACKNOWLEDGMENTS

My thanks to the team at Twelve for all their help on this second adventure together. Sean Desmond has a rare gift for inspiring an author to embrace a new project, and then further convincing them to maintain that enthusiasm. (Even on the third draft.) My gratitude to Jay Mandel at William Morris Endeavour for the encouragement and for making things happen.

I am fortunate to work for a company that stands behind its reporters. I'm also blessed to work with so many talented journalists at the *WSJ* editorial pages. A special salute to Paul Gigot, for so steadily leading our pages in these political times. Also a shout-out to William McGurn and Holman Jenkins, for their own insightful reporting on the Russia-collusion saga.

Throughout that saga, only a handful of reporters and analysts proved willing to buck the conventional wisdom. We all learned a lot from each other, and I am grateful for this broader group's efforts. They include Byron York at the *Washington Examiner*, Mollie Hemingway at *The Federalist*, Andrew McCarthy at *National Review*, Chuck Ross at the Daily Caller News Foundation, Catherine Herridge at Fox News, John Solomon at *The Hill*, and Sara Carter. My thanks, too, for the many Fox News hosts who made a point of spreading the truth.

I'm fortunate over the years to have developed a network of Washington sources who are smart, dogged, and honest. They can't be named here, but I am immensely appreciative of their investigative work and their willingness to trust me with their findings.

My youngest sister ordered me to acknowledge her by name in this book, and as usual she is getting what she wants. (Kidding, kidding.) Thank you, Tish, and Kandis, and Julie, for the Facetime chats and calls that always make me wish I was in Oregon, and glad I have never tried pineapple vodka. Mom, you are the best. Your cheerful outlook and work ethic are both inspirations, and they always encourage me to push on a few more hours.

My warmest thanks go to my nearest and dearest. My crazy world would not work without the hourly love and support of Nicholas Van Dyke, my husband. For every hour I put into this book, he put in several more managing home, work, and children. He has the harder job, and yet he does it with extraordinary cheer.

As for those remarkable kids: It was late March 2019, when my youngest child finally lost patience. Mueller filed his report on a Friday, requiring me to (once again) halt weekend plans, this time to go on TV. The seven-year-old sat down to pen an outraged letter. "Dear Bob Mueller," she printed. "You ruined my weekend. We were at our cabin, but had to get up early and leave so Mom could work. Also, thanks to you, we weren't able to get our new puppy. Try doing your work on a Tuesday!!!"

Between the special counsel and this book, my children have had less mom-time than they would probably like. But they are the most understanding of kiddos and consummate good sports. Oliver, Stella, and Frances—thank you.

INDEX

ABOUT THE AUTHOR

Kimberley Strassel is a member of the editorial board of the *Wall Street Journal*. She writes editorials as well as the weekly "Potomac Watch" column about politics. Ms. Strassel joined Dow Jones & Company in 1994, working in the news department of the *Wall Street Journal Europe* in Brussels and then in London. She moved to New York in 1999 and soon thereafter joined the *Journal*'s editorial page, working as a features editor and then as an editorial writer. She assumed her current position in 2005. She is a Fox News contributor, a 2014 Bradley Price recipient, and the author of the national bestseller *The Intimidation Game: How the Left Is Silencing Free Speech*. An Oregon native, she attended Princeton University.